LET GO OF THE SHORE

For years I have loved Karen Drucker's music, spirit, heart, talent, humor, wisdom, authenticity, and service. Now I love her book. In *Let Go of the Shore*, Karen will touch you with her stories, tickle you with her humor, move you with her wisdom, and make you feel like she's your best friend. How lucky can you get?

— **ALAN COHEN**, author of *A Deep Breath of Life*

Karen Drucker is a musical genius and her marvelous book expands that genius into writing that is uplifting, touching and profound. How absolutely deluxe to have this book!

— **SARK**, artist, author of *Succulent Wild Woman*

Through stories and songs where she reveals her foibles and flaws as well as her passionate embrace of life, Karen Drucker inspires us not just to accept ourselves as we are, but to squeeze every drop of joy from our days. And did I mention she's funny? A must read for anyone who ever considered themselves odd or different—and that's all of us.

— **M.J. RYAN**, author of *Attitudes of Gratitude*

Karen Drucker's stories, like her music, are full of deep hearted wisdom, gentle but ruthless honesty and uplifting humour. She teaches us how to keep our hearts open and how to make a difference in the world without taking ourselves too seriously. If you want to embrace your humanness and open yourself to the kind of truths we need to hear each day read *Let Go of the Shore*. These are stories to savour and return to again and again.

— **ORIAH MOUNTAIN DREAMER,**
author of *The Invitation*

In all my travels to the leading new paradigm healing conferences of the last 20 years, no one has inspired me like Karen Drucker... Karen is a musical and spiritual genius.

— **CANDACE PERT, PHD,** author of *EverythingYou Need to Know to Feel Go(o)d.*

LET GO OF THE SHORE

*Stories and Songs That Set
the Spirit Free*

Karen Drucker

DeVorss Publications
Camarillo, California

Let Go of the Shore BOOK ISBN: 9780875168531

SECOND PRINTING, 2024

DeVorss & Company, Publisher
P.O. Box 1389
Camarillo CA 93011-1389
www.devorss.com

Printed in the United States of America

Library of Congress Cataloging-in-Publication Data

Drucker, Karen, 1957-
  Let go of the shore : stories and songs that set the spirit free / Karen Drucker.
    p. cm.
Includes discography and index.
ISBN 978-0-87516-853-1 (pbk.: alk. paper) 1. Drucker, Karen, 1957-
2. Singers—United States—Biography. 3. Inspiration. I. Title.
  ML420.D87A3 2010
  782.42092—dc22
  [B]
                                                                2009051704

TABLE OF CONTENTS

Part Three: Let It Shine

DEDICATION

To Johnny: Whenever I would let go of one shore for another, you would always be the angel on my shoulder saying I could do it. Your love is a gift that I treasure in my heart every day.

THANK YOU

To those of you who laughed at me, thank you,
without you I wouldn't have cried.
To those of you who just couldn't love me, thank you,
without you I wouldn't have known real love.
To those of you who hurt my feelings, thank you,
without you I wouldn't have felt them.
To those of you who left me lonely, thank you,
without you I wouldn't have discovered myself.
But those of you who thought I couldn't do it,
it is you I thank the most,
because without you
I wouldn't have tried.

ANONYMOUS

Thank you to ALL my friends, and the people I have met along my path. You have all graced my life and I have received gifts from every one of you.

A special thank you to:

My parents, Marjorie and Murray Drucker, who showed me by example what it means to live life on your own terms and whose love, wisdom and support have shaped who I am today.

My sister, Tina, who is my friend and inspiration.

John Hoy, for years ago encouraging and helping me to record my very first CD (and every one since then!) and to write this book, and for all the ways you love and support me. I never take a day with you for granted. You are the blessing in my life.

Maye Cavallaro, for laughs, food, more laughs and a wonderfully supportive, creative, fun and fabulous friendship.

Rev. David Ault, for being my friend and mentor, and seeing

a bigger vision of myself and always cheerleading me towards it. I am so grateful for you in my life.

Joan Borysenko, for such love and support and being a great sis! I think our meeting was divinely created and I am blessed by our friendship.

SARK, for our almost daily phone calls of love, laughter and encouragement. You model to me what living in joy looks like!

Alan Cohen, for being my supportive, loveable, big brother, and teaching me about what "Is It and Not It"… and you, my friend—are "It"!

Annie Stocking, for singing with me since we were 19 years old, and arranging every back-up part on every song I have ever written! My "sound" on every CD is a direct result of you and John and I am so grateful!

My author friends who have been an inspiration, and provided the tools to help me live an authentic life: M.J. Ryan, Cheri Huber, Mary Manin Morrisey, Oriah Mountain Dreamer, Debbie Ford, Cheryl Richardson, Candice Pert.

To my friends through the years who are always there for me and keep me laughing: Eddie Conner, Rev. David Leonard, Janet Carol Ryan, Jennifer Mann, Lisa Smith, Rev. Karyl Huntley, Jennifer Lacy, Jessica Jones, Lauren Mayer, Maggie Cole, April Ortiz, Frank Darabont, Melinda Moore, Allen Yamashita, Robyn Posin.

Sue Faria for the first round of editing this book, and for helping with all the details of my life. I am so grateful for all your help.

Kathy Juline for final editing and for being so encouraging.

Brian Narelle for your perfect cartoons—you added so much!

Melinda Grubbauer and Gary Peattie from DeVorss Publishing, thank you for this amazing opportunity.

My fellow swimmers from Tiburon Peninsula Masters Swimming, especially my coaches Ken DeMont and "Mean" Mike McDonald, and my cold-water-loving friends at the Dolphin Club of San Francisco.

To all my fellow New Thought musician peers: Thank you for

gracing me and inspiring me with your talent. Let's all keep supporting each other to get our positive music out into the world!

To all the New Thought churches, ministers, workshop leaders, and authors who have supported my music, played my CDs in your classes, workshops, or retreats, had me sing and speak at your churches—thank you for helping me spread my message of positive, affirmative music, and for helping me live my dream.

To all the people who have used my music in their personal lives and especially those who have used it for their own healing…what an honor to accompany you on your path.

Gone but never forgotten: Brian Connolly

SPECIAL
ACKNOWLEDGEMENTS

Graphics: Lisa Winger

Illustrations: Brian Narelle

Back cover photo: Carl Studna

INTRODUCTION

It all started with a woman coming up to my table wanting to buy a CD after one of my concerts. She scanned my table, and after asking me questions about each of my CDs, finally said, "And what about your book? Did you already sell out? Can I order it on Amazon?" After the initial shock that this was now the fifth person in the last week who had asked me the same question, I had to ponder my answer. Ever since that seed was planted (without my even knowing there was fertile soil, where it was planted) the Universe has been trying to get my attention. I laughed about how this kind of thing works. I have seen in my life that whenever there was a next step for me to do, Spirit (or God, The Universe, Source — whatever you want to call it) would just keep gently tapping me on the shoulder in a manner like this, getting my attention to let me know it was just "time." Time to move on from something, or time to make a change. Time to be quiet, or time to take a risk and go for it. This time it was about writing a book.

I have been so blessed to perform my music with many well-known authors in the New Thought field, so I have to admit it was a bit intimidating to even think I could undertake writing a book. Did I have any talent for it, and could I actually finish it? Would my inner critic have her way with me by asking, "Who do you think you are to write a book? Who cares what you have to say. Besides it's all been said before! Just stick to writing songs!" But when I look back, I realize that so much of the joy in my life has always been from stretching, growing and trying new things. That is what this book is for me. I have loved the creative process of writing these stories (many of them on airplanes traveling around the country to my various gigs), and searching my heart to say what was real for me. So, as I have done so many times before, I let my inner critic rant and rave, and then simply sat down and started writing.

I am not trying to set the world on fire with my words or dispense precious advice about how to live your life or how to become a millionaire in three quick and easy steps. I just have some stories and songs, and some insights that I have learned that might possibly resonate with you and maybe provoke a few "Aha" moments… and that is my favorite part of life. It's those moments when I read something or hear a song, or someone tells me a story, and I just "get it," and feel those "God-bumps" that tingle from my head to my toes. Maybe you will see some of yourself in my stories and we can have a connection through our learning of life's lessons and navigating the tides.

So settle back, make a cup of tea, and spend some time with me. I hope you'll be glad that you did.

Karen

Authoring Your Own Best Life

Joan Borysenko, Ph.D.

> It was the best of times, it was the worst of times,
> it was the age of wisdom, it was the age of foolishness,
> it was the epoch of belief, it was the epoch of incredulity,
> it was the season of Light, it was the season of Darkness,
> it was the spring of hope, it was the winter of despair…
> CHARLES DICKENS, *A Tale of Two Cities*

> Ain't it the truth. And that's why we need Karen Drucker so much in
> the times we are living in now.
> JOAN BORYSENKO, *A Tale of Two Friends*

As an author of fourteen books I know what a challenge it is to write in the authentic, engaging (and refreshingly real and funny) style of the book you now hold in your hands. Each story that you will read in these pages is like a pearl, strung on the thread of essential human goodness that is Karen Drucker.

An inspired life is all about overcoming our circumstances and apparent limitations so that we can follow the promptings of our own best self as it calls to us. In Karen's words, it's about letting go of the shore. That means cultivating the trust to allow the current of spirit to direct us. That's what Karen's life and music are all about.

Let me add one more pearl to Karen's string and tell you a story (A Tale of Two Friends) about how her music and her presence transform lives and transcend differences. It is a mild, sunshiny day in Phoenix, Arizona, in November of 2008. But inner storms are brewing. Emotions at the New Thought conference where Karen and I are both presenters are running high.

Barack Obama has just been elected the 44th President of the United States after a hotly contested, volatile, and divisive campaign. And Phoenix is the home turf of war hero John McCain, who has lost the election by an unexpected margin. The tide is turning and the waters are troubled.

A mood of ecstatic jubilation emanates from the Obama supporters who are the majority of the two thousand conference attendees gathered for a weekend of practical and spiritual inspiration. But an undercurrent of grief and disappointment ripples through the air of the auditorium. The tension between the two emotional poles—and the people who are broadcasting these feelings—is electric. It begs a question deeply relevant to the destiny of our planet in these turbulent times. Can we open our hearts to those with different beliefs, coming closer to one another through a shared desire for mutual understanding...or not?

My first impulse (a neurological tic inherited from my anxious Jewish mother) is to cut and run. Conference be darned, I want to go home and chill out. Misunderstandings and difficulties are surely in the offing. But at the same time the grown up part of me knows that those potential difficulties are an opportunity to face fear, overcome differences, and connect to one another through our shared hope for a better future. How best to do that? Not by talking surely—at least at first. Our hearts have to be softened and opened before we can see each other rightly.

Enter the Divine Miss Karen, the Queen of Hearts. (I'm sure that she's blushing as she reads these words, although as you'll read in one of her delightful stories, she is a practitioner of the gracious art of accepting praise). Who better to open a conference, I think, I hope. It's a tough gig for sure.

With her mane of luxuriant red hair flowing, Karen steps into the spotlight and begins to sing some of the songs she'll introduce you to in these pages. In just a few minutes we are all (well, most of us anyway) laughing. Karen is one of the funniest people you will ever meet and it takes a devoted sourpuss to resist her humor.

Then we are all (well, most of us anyway) crying, touched to the core by her uncanny ability to evoke the best in us—our deepest human capacities for kindness, hope, and love. Above all, Karen sings the diverse group into safety, into that place inside where preferences dissolve and everything is okay just as it is. We take a collective breath. And in letting go and breathing deeply and naturally, as she describes in the lyrics to her song "Breathe," the door to healing opens.

Heal, comfort, inspire, evoke, and guide us to our own inner strength and wisdom. This is what Karen does. She is an authentic spiritual teacher although she's far too humble to call herself that. The gift she gives is uncontrived. It is her own best self, which shines.

Every one of us needs a friend who can encourage and support us in our growth toward compassion, wisdom, and happiness. Without minimizing life's difficulties or sliding into glib optimism, Karen helps us look beneath the surface of life's challenges so that we can discover the jewel hidden in the depths. The spontaneous mantra that kept repeating itself to me as I read each of her heartfelt, real, and funny stories was, "Karen is a truly good human being, a model for us all." The wisdom that she is inhabits her music and comes alive inside the listener. If that's not magic, I don't know what is.

The great hope of our time is that open hearts will pave the way for open minds. And open minds will collaborate to create a future that is just and compassionate for all. Karen's gift is her ability to heal and open hearts.

LET GO OF THE SHORE

Part One:
I Can Do It

I Can Do It

Growing up in Hollywood, I often felt there must be some-thing in the drinking water that made me obsessed with my looks. You could be the most intelligent, warm, caring person, but all that seemed to matter was your physical attractiveness. Hollywood was where movie stars lived, where movies were made, and it was part of the culture to feel enormous pressure about your physical appearance, even from a very early age.

As a kid, I had friends who were the sons or daughters of movie stars, of studio executives, or of someone who knew someone who was a really big cheese. It was all about being "someone." If you had the perfect size 2, tanned body, and long blond straight hair— well, then you were "in." (It also helped if your name was something like Shannon, Britney, or Buffy.) If, on the other hand, you had acne, braces, and curly, frizzy hair you tried to straighten to look like the long blonde types—well, you just didn't make the grade.

But, oh, how I tried.

I was a total geek. I had acne and braces. I was 5 foot 7 inches in the 6th grade, fully developed, and I did everything humanly possible to flatten down my breasts and straighten my hair. Remember Dippity Do? I would glob the stuff on my hair every night, wrap up one side of my hair with a million bobby pins, wrap up the other side with even more bobby pins, wrap the remaining hair on top around an orange juice can, and pray to God that by morning my hair would be straight. It never was. Heaven forbid if it was ever foggy in Los Angeles, my hair would rise like yeast and my secret would be out.

The one thing I did have going for me was that I was funny. I started to understand that my sense of humor was actually opening doors for me in the ever-important world of "cliques" in junior high school and that people actually seemed to like me. I started to be accepted into the "in" crowd simply because I was funny. The cute girls were never threatened by me because there was no way I would steal their boyfriends. The cute guys at school, who had ignored me before, began to treat me like I was "one of the guys" because I made them laugh. I was a jock, and they could relate to me in a way that they couldn't with the pretty girls.

But that was the ultimate—to be a pretty girl. I yearned to feel that I looked good, that I was worthy, that I was accepted. I laugh at this now because I remember a time in my twenties when I probably did have that "perfect" body from doing so many big swim events and triathlons, but because of feeling unworthy I hid my body under bulky clothes. If only I could have loved and accepted myself then.

When I was in junior high I found someone I could admire, someone who gave me faith and hope. She had a background like mine, had gone to my same school, and made me feel like anything was possible. Her name? Carol Burnett. I loved Carol Burnett. I still do, but when I was thirteen she was everything to me. I watched her show religiously, memorized her funniest monologues, and even learned how to do the Tarzan call that she was famous for. She was my role model, mentor, and a shining star that showed me a way to accept myself at a time when I felt like such an outcast. Her story and success inspired me, and I was a tried and true fan.

She taped her television show at CBS Television Studios right down the street from my school. Every Friday I had this ritual where I would leave school at 3:00 pm, take the bus down to the CBS Television Studios, and wait in line every week to get tickets for the afternoon taping of "The Carol Burnett Show." I would wear the same little checkered dress my mom had made for me, and make a beeline for the same seat in the front row. I did this with such regularity that eventually she would see me and give me a special "I know you" wink that made me feel like I was special. It didn't matter that I was a geek and not as pretty as the other girls at school. Carol Burnett had winked at ME!

She always started her show with a question and answer period with the audience. On this particular day, I am just sitting there listening to everyone ask their questions when out of the blue, I feel my heart start to race and I look down and notice that my palms are getting all sweaty. I have no idea what is happening to me until all of a sudden, as if possessed by some demon, I witness my right hand shoot up, and before I can pull it back down, she calls on me. With my heart racing and barely able to speak, I say in a timid voice, "Um... I would like to challenge you to a Tarzan Calling Contest." She gives a startled look, but the audience applauds loudly, so she invites me up on stage to do the challenge. The next moment I am standing next to my idol, on national television! But then I see them. A whole gang of the cool girls from my school are sitting in the sixth row, rolling their eyes, laughing and whispering. I know they are saying in their most exaggerated Valley Girl accents, "Oh My Gawd! Isn't that, like, Karen Drucker, that geekie girl from Mrs. Spiegleman's class? Oh she is, like, so weird! What is she doing up there?" I feel myself start to close down, wondering how in the world I got myself into this situation and how I can get myself out of it. But here I am. A decision has to be made in a split second: close down and stay safe, or risk it all and go for it. Something deep inside of me says "Yes!" I choose to go for it.

I went first. I took a deep breath, let out my best Tarzan call, and was greeted enthusiastically by the audience. I was in heaven.

I was on stage performing with Carol Burnett! I was funny and people were laughing. The poor sound guy must have gotten his ears blown out because he had lowered the microphone down low, thinking that as a kid I wouldn't be very loud. But I was. Then Carol did her Tarzan call. Being the gracious hostess she was, she bowed to me like I was the better Tarzan caller and the audience went nuts.

I sat down in my seat, and knew that I had just crossed over a threshold that would forever change the way I saw myself. I had made the choice to "go for it," to risk, to grow, to step out of my comfort zone. The next day in school I saw the "cool girls" who had intimidated me so much, and now they treated me differently. I had been seen. I had stepped up and stepped out, and I had allowed myself to shine. I loved the feeling of moving past my sweaty palms and thumping heartbeat to get to the other side to complete exhilaration and self-fulfillment. I was hooked, and for me this was just the beginning.

"Whether you think you can do a thing or think you can't, you're right"

HENRY FORD

I Can Do It

Words: Karen Drucker
Music: Karen Drucker & John Hoy

CHORUS:
I can do it. I can do anything.
When I say what I want and I walk my talk,
it all comes back to me.
I can do it. I can do anything.
I release. Let go. Go with the flow.
This is where I'm supposed to be.

Today I say I'll get out of my way,
and live the life that's meant for me.
I state my claim in Spirit's name.
I choose my destiny.

CHORUS

Right here, right now, today I choose how,
to be all I can be.
I can heal my life, let go of the strife.
I embrace the mystery.

CHORUS

CHAPTER 2

Just Do It

Swimming was all I knew how to do. Spending my youth as a competitive swimmer, I never had the time to cultivate any other interests. But, oh, if they only knew! I harbored a great desire to sing. To act. To just be on stage where that magic light would hit a person and she would be transformed into someone different, someone special. I cut out pictures and articles about the stars I admired—Bette Midler, Barbra Streisand, Liza Minnelli, Carol Burnett. I felt this desire was an enormous secret I had to hold close to my heart. I was so afraid that my family and friends would laugh at me if I revealed how much I wanted to be up on stage, so I played make believe.

When I was in my early teens, I lived for those moments when everyone was out of the house and I would be home alone to play out my fantasy. I would take out my Barbra Streisand albums and my hairbrush (to use for a microphone), stick my mom's long wig on my head (so I could pretend I had long, straight hair) and lip-synch in front of the mirror to all the albums. I would do this for hours, imagining, pretending that I was up on stage and that I had talent. Every five minutes or so I would look out the window to make sure that my parents weren't coming in the driveway. When I heard the sound of the car backing in, I would immediately turn off the music, throw the wig and the "mic" in my secret stash place, and pretend that I had been studying the whole time. God forbid if they ever found out what I was actually doing!

This "secret life" went on all through junior high. When I entered the famed Hollywood High School with its renowned music and theater department, I knew I had to finally just go for it. Mustering up every ounce of courage I had, I set an audition date to join the choir and kept it a secret. With my knees knocking, heart thumping, and voice definitely tight and quivering, I sang a few little songs for the choir director. He looked up at me, looked down at his yellow pad where he was scribbling some notes, and simply said, "Karen, I think you should stick to swimming." I was crushed. He had no clue that it took every ounce of courage to stand before him and be that vulnerable. Most choirs just want as many voices as they can get to make a big sound, and here I was being rejected and told I couldn't sing. I was humiliated and depressed. I locked away my secret desire to sing and went back to swimming.

A year later, at the start of my sophomore year at Hollywood High, a weird turn of events happened. The older choir director who had rejected me the year before had recently died. A new teacher, Glen Hubbard, had just been hired and was auditioning kids for the choir. Could I go through that humiliation again? Was I really as bad as the last teacher had thought? I knew I couldn't live with myself if I didn't give it just one more try, so I set the date for my audition.

With the exact same physical sensations of knees knocking, heart thumping and voice quivering that I had felt the year before, I sang my little songs for Mr. Hubbard. Smiling warmly at me, he said, "Karen, you have a lovely voice, why did it take you so long to audition?" I felt like the hand of God had just touched me, the sky had opened up, and the angels started singing. As far as I know I probably sang horribly that day, but Mr. Hubbard saw something in me that gave me the confidence to at least try.

I threw myself into music, teaching myself to play piano, singing at every school function, and writing little songs of teenage angst.

With my newfound confidence, I even auditioned for the Hollywood High School marching band — as a drummer! When the marching band teacher said to me, "Girls can't play drums," that was my invitation to prove him wrong. For three months before my audition, I practiced daily how to read drum music, and marched up and down my street getting used to the weight of the heavy drum. When my audition day came I was ready and I aced it. He had no choice but to let me into the drum corps. I was the first girl in H.H.S history to play drums in the marching band. At first the boys were not thrilled to let me into their "club" but when they saw my dedication and ability, over time I was accepted and loved playing at every football game.

I had made a friend in the choir who I thought was the epitome of "cool." Melinda had long blond curly hair, wore funky velvet coats and platform shoes, and would sit at the piano and sing. She was poised and confident, and she knew about getting gigs in the world outside of school. She asked me to sing back-ups for her at the world famous folk club of the 70's called the Troubadour. It would be my first "gig" ever and I was thrilled. I was sixteen years old and could not believe I was going to live out my fantasy of being a singer. We practiced some Paul Williams ballads and I was really excited about the prospect of actually being up on stage. The performance was scary and exciting, and it planted a seed in me like an addiction. I craved the challenge of doing something on my own.

I found out that the Troubadour had "Hoot Nights" every Monday night, where anyone could come down and perform for free. The deal was you would sign up at 3:00 p.m. on Monday afternoon and they would usually take between three and five performers to be the opening act for the headliner that night. I practiced for weeks, even wrote a few original songs, and set the date to go down and have my big chance at stardom.

When I got there on that fateful Monday there was a long line of aspiring "stars"-hippies with guitars, women with skirts to their ankles and long flowing hair, and people who looked as if they had been camping for weeks. I learned my first lesson in show biz: determination and stamina. I learned that this was a waiting game, that even though they said you could come at 3:00 p.m. to sign up for that night's show, only those who came early would actually get the coveted slots. Because of this, people kept coming earlier and earlier. That first day I came I didn't get on, or the next week, or the next week. No matter how early I arrived, there would already be several people in line in front of me. If I was the fourth person in line I would play the game that maybe one of the top three might not make it to the end of the day, that at some point someone would throw in the towel. Or maybe I would get lucky and they'd want two guys and a gal - and I would get in after all.

After weeks of psyching up and dealing with the disappointment of not having my turn at stardom, I decided it was time for drastic measures. I set my alarm clock, packed a lunch and water, brought a blanket and a few books along with some songs to write, and got there at 8:00 a.m. in the morning! To my amazement I was first in line, and within minutes, five more hardy souls joined me. We shared stories, sang songs, and became friends, all the while psyching one other out to see who would make it through the long marathon day.

Finally at 3:00 p.m., the door opened, bringing with it the smell of beer and cigarettes and a peek into the dark room with the large stage. My heart began to race as the cigarette-smoking, jaded bartender who was given this job took down my name and said, "Okay, kid, be back at 7:30 for an 8:00 show. You have three songs or 12 minutes, whichever comes first."

I raced home with a mixture of fear, anxiety, and pure adrenaline to get ready for my night. I did my three songs (timed perfectly so I wouldn't get the red light that says, "Get the hell off the stage, your time is up!") and even though I was pretty bad and I'm sure I was singing off key a lot of the time, my parents and friends gave me credit for having the guts to get up there in the first place.

I was so excited with the idea of getting better and learning how to work with all the butterflies in my stomach that this marathon routine of getting booked at the Troubadour became a regular activity all through high school. I found out about other "Hoot Nights" at local folk clubs like the world famous Ice House in Pasadena and a small club called 2 Dollar Bills. Aside from the fact that I didn't realize it was a gay bar, they had a piano that whenever I would play with any gusto, the ivory from the keys would actually fly off the piano, sometimes hitting me in the face.

I also tried out for our high school talent shows, although they terrified me. Hollywood High School was known for its talent and I felt much safer playing (and being bad) in places where no one knew who I was. Playing before my peers was a whole other issue. I auditioned for one show that was held up the street at the Holiday Inn. They had a round circular stage about five feet off the ground, with the piano to the far right so there would be room for all of the singers and dancers who had to fit on the small circle. When I got up to sing and went to the piano, I hadn't realized that the piano bench was placed within one inch of the end of the stage. I sat down, smiled to the audience, adjusted the piano bench, and immediately fell backwards, with my legs going up into the air in a kind of creative gymnastics split. Maybe that's when I unintentionally began my comedy career.

I found one thing to be true for me in all these years of being a musician—I just had to do it. I had to show up and just keep showing up. I had something inside of me that needed to be expressed, and even when I was not any good and was scared out of my wits, I just kept showing up and doing it. I played anywhere and everywhere, and was greedy for any kind of experience that I could get. I loved singing, I loved music, and I loved performing. I never waited until I was ready, or perfect, or even until I thought I was any good. Even now after making my living doing this for so many years, I still question if I am good enough, or if a song of mine is well written, or if my next CD will sell. But I love the quote from Martha Graham, who said: "It is not your business to determine how good (your talent) is, nor how it compares .... It is your business to keep the channel open. You do not even have to believe in yourself or your work. You have to keep open and aware to the urges that motivate you."

So that is what I try to do, just keep open, just keep growing, just keep doing it.

P.S. Mr. Hubbard passed away a few years ago. I am grateful to have known him. I give him such credit for seeing my light and allowing me the opportunity to shine.

"All things are coming to you...don't argue about it, just do it."
ERNEST HOLMES

Just Do It

Words: Karen Drucker
Music: Karen Drucker & John Hoy

Just do it. Don't talk about it. Don't put if off. Just do it.
Just say it. I'll speak my truth. I'll state my needs. Just say it.
Just claim it. Act as if. Know it's done. Just claim it.
Just breathe. Breathe in faith. Breathe out fear. Just breathe.

CHORUS:
Just do it! Just do it! Just do it! Just do it! Just do it!
I'm gonna give myself a gentle push, I'm gonna start today!

Just do it. Don't talk about it. Don't put it off. Just do it.
Just trust. Trust myself. Trust my heart. Just trust.
Love. I'm gonna give love. I'm gonna show love. Just love.
Faith. I have faith. All is well. I have faith.

CHORUS

RAP:
Every time I criticize and focus on my flaws,
I don't realize that I am worthy and capable,
and I deserve to have it all!
So now's my time to rise and shine,
go for the dreams that are in my mind.
Take one small step and not be afraid,
with faith and love I've got it made!

CHORUS:
Just do it! Just do it! Just do it! Just do it! Just do it!
I'm gonna give myself a gentle push, I'm gonna start today!
Just do it. It's done!

CHAPTER 3

We Are the Ones That We've Been Waiting For

I never realized what a unique and different childhood I had until I went away to college. As a teenager growing up in the Hollywood Hills, I would hike after school with my two dogs and sit gazing out at the legendary Hollywood Sign, imagining all the stories that went along with old Hollywood.

The Hollywood sign was falling into disrepair and when I heard they were planning to tear it down due to lack of funds, I was shocked. How could this be? The sign was a symbol of Hollywood and the movies, and people travel from all over the world to see this landmark. The thirteen-year-old entrepreneur in me knew I had to do something. I still don't know what possessed me to do this, but I decided to organize a bike ride to raise the funds to save the sign. Now that I look back on this idea, I have so much admiration for the naiveté of kids. Raising the hundreds of thousands of dollars this project would cost was not even in my realm of thinking. I just knew that they wanted to tear down my sign, and it was up to ME to save it!

I gathered all my friends together and explained the whole plan for the bike ride. Everyone took on jobs including publicity, mapping out the bike course, making up the pledge forms, and getting our junior high school on board. I had the idea that if we could have some big name stars show up at the start of the ride, it would generate more interest. I wrote letters to a bunch of stars, with no luck. When I went to the taping of the Carol Burnett Show, I sent a letter backstage to her. I got a nice rejection letter back. Somehow, however, through some of these contacts, I got my star for the day: "Ms. Hollywood." I had no idea who she was, but it looked good on the flyer. A few local TV stations even promised they would show up and cover the event.

The day came for the bike ride, and about a hundred kids showed up with bikes and pledge forms from $20 to $100. Fifteen minutes before the ride was supposed to start, a vision in skin-tight hot pink hot pants, purple spandex tube top, and chunky platform heels, walked towards me. She had Dolly Parton hair and breasts the size of watermelons. Just about every kid fell off their bike watching her. Our school was located right below Hollywood Boulevard with its interesting "characters," to say the least, and my first thought was that one of the "locals" was going to create a scene at our event. She came up to me, extended her hand, with its long, pink fake fingernails, and in a voice just like that of Marilyn Monroe, said, "Hi, honey. I am Ms. Hollywood, and I am here to help you save the sign!" The kid in me was a bit shocked, but the producer in me knew the media would love this. Ms. Hollywood was a guarantee that we would make the evening news.

At the appointed time the bikers got into place, Ms. Hollywood lifted the flag, and in a surprisingly drill sergeant-type manner let rip a "Ready, Set, Go!" The kids were off, the media got their footage, and I started adding up the pledge forms.

Everyone had a good time, and on Monday morning I triumphantly walked into the Hollywood Chamber of Commerce to drop off a big pile of cash, reveling in the knowledge that we had saved the sign! When the clerk counted out the seven hundred dollars we raised, she gave me a look of pity mixed with motherly pride. She gently explained that it would take a whole lot more money to save the sign and that I should still feel good for at least trying.

I walked out of there feeling dejected and depressed. I felt like I had failed all the kids who had joined me in this project. After lots of "Well, we tried," we all moved on and waited for the announcement of when the sign would be torn down.

As with most things political and civic, the actual planning of the demolition of the sign took months, with all the red tape and the bidding wars to determine who would do it. The delays gave local businesses time to join forces and eventually, because of all the publicity and heated debates about the importance of this icon, enough money was raised and the sign was saved after all. The Hollywood Chamber of Commerce gave me a little plaque for my efforts, and I found out that the two main businesses that contributed the most money heard about the need to save the Hollywood sign through our bike ride.

I realize now, so many years later, what a gift that whole experience was to me. I love the quote from Mother Theresa: "We cannot do great things, only small things with great love," and also Gandhi's quote: "Be the change you wish to see in the world." Even though I am sure my parents and teachers knew that whatever money we could raise would just be a drop in the bucket compared to the amount needed to save the sign, they encouraged all of us to do whatever we could. I think I am still living like this today. I want to be a person who makes a difference, and I try to do what I can to be the change I want to see in the world.

And the Hollywood sign? It's still there, presiding over an ever-changing city, regal and shining. Whenever I go home, I look at it and just smile.

"Now is the time and we are the ones that we've been waiting for."
HOPI ELDERS

We Are the Ones

Words & Music: Karen Drucker

CHORUS:
We are the ones that we've been waiting for.
We are the ones who will make a difference.
We are the ones who will change the world.
We are the ones, we are, we are.
We are the ones, we are, we are.

I've been feelin' like I can't make a difference.
Been feelin' like there ain't no use.
Feelin' tired and a little unconscious,
coming up with every kind of excuse.
'Till I realized it's not all up to me,
when we join together we shape our destiny,
to see a world where we are living as one.
It can be, it shall be, it will be done.

CHORUS

No one else gonna' make the changes.
No savior gonna' drop from the sky.
Nothin' left to do but wake up, 'cause it's really up to you and I.
To take it one step at a time,
stand together with your hand in mine.
Then we will see the world that we've been dreaming about,
we need it now, the time is now, there is no doubt.

CHORUS

CHAPTER 4

Prosperity

It's not so much that I am cheap — let's just say I have had a lot of practice in taking the "more economical route." I come from a family that lived by the motto, "If you can't buy it wholesale, it's not worth buying." During the years I was growing up in the Southern California area, my father owned a fashion magazine called *The California Girl,* in which all of the different clothing designers would showcase their new fall line for the wholesale market of retailers. In other words, this was a magazine for people in the fashion trade and not a magazine you would find on a newsstand.

My childhood was spent either going to fashion shows at the California Mart in downtown Los Angeles where all the clothing buyers would display their clothes or, in sharp contrast, going to dog shows. Aside from *The California Girl*, my parents also published three show-dog magazines: *The Collie Review, The Boxer Review,* and *The Cocker Spaniel Review.* My parents were independent, self-made entrepreneurs and worked very hard for their money. I still can hear my mother's IBM Selectric typewriter humming away, setting the copy for the magazines, as I woke up (this was way before computers, which later on made her job so much easier). My father would leave at the crack of dawn to brave the gridlock traffic to drive to downtown L.A. and did not return until late at night. We always had what we needed, but the message was clear — we only had just what we needed. If I wanted any new clothes, they were either made by my mother (how she found the time to do this and put out her monthly magazines I don't know), or purchased off the rack from some local children's manufacturer who had stock left over from last year.

We rarely had normal family vacations. All of the trips we ever took were business related, where my dad was able to score free seats on an airplane or get hotel rooms by trading for an ad in his magazine. Everything was a deal, and I learned from hearing him on the phone how to wheel-and-deal anything and everything. One of his favorite stories is how he wined and dined my mother when they were first dating by taking her to all the fanciest restaurants in town where everyone knew him by name. It turns out that these were all restaurants where, in exchange for an ad in his magazine, all he had to do was leave a ten-dollar tip to look like a big spender.

So it makes sense that as I grew up I took on the same mentality around money. I always knew that it was up to me to work for everything I wanted, starting at an early age. When I was about eight years old, my entrepreneurial spirit was in full bloom. While other kids were enjoying their summer vacation, I set up an elaborate lemonade stand with flashing lights and a huge colorful sign, fully intending to be rich by the end of the summer. They say that "location is everything," but it never occurred to me that we lived on a street where there was hardly any traffic. Maybe one or two cars per hour. I made about 75 cents that first day mainly from my neighbors coming out to get their mail and taking pity on this poor pathetic kid. (To this day, I always stop whenever I see any kid selling lemonade!)

I had my first "real" job when I was twelve years old, working at Beverly Hills Ponyland. This was a run-down little stable with a dozen or so miniature ponies that would simply walk around in a predetermined circle with the child sitting on top of the pony, waving to their parents. My job was to walk behind the ponies and scoop up their droppings as soon as they did their business. Since the main clientele were the children of famous movie stars, the owner made sure that no one would ever see or smell anything foul—so there I was scooping away for twelve hours a day! I made about $10 a day and was thrilled with my financial independence.

When I became a teenager my material aspirations grew. Now I had my sights set on something specific: a fancy ten-speed bicycle.

When I asked my parents for a new bike, they told me to figure out how I could get the money for it. The purple one with the flames on it was one hundred dollars, and I wanted it! So I did the logical thing — I went up and down my street asking each neighbor if they had any odd jobs I could do for them that summer to pay for my bike. Growing up in Laurel Canyon in the late 60's and early 70's, I was surrounded by a surge of young, hip musicians, actors, and directors living in my neighborhood, and some of them helped me in my quest. I got a few odd jobs, but the job that stood out was walking Denny Doherty's (Papa Denny from the Mamas and the Papas) English Sheep dogs. These were big, furry, slobbery, and untrained dogs that would immediately drag you along for the ride as soon as a leash was on them. The plan was that I would go over every day after summer school, put their leashes on, and walk them for twenty minutes.

At the end of the first week of doing my job, Denny asked me to come into the house. I thought I was being fired. I wanted that bike so much, and had thought that doing this job for two months would get me my hundred dollars. Well, he pulled out a crisp hundred-dollar bill and said, "You did a good job, kid — now go and get that bike!" I was elated. This was easy, and it had only taken me a week! I still remember looking back as I ran home, holding that hundred dollar bill like it was a precious diamond, and seeing Denny standing on his balcony looking down at me with the sweetest smile.

Sure enough, I got my bike. However, my father wanted to teach me a lesson about money and commitments, and made me go back anyway and walk those dogs for the rest of the summer.

As I grew into my twenties and started making my living as a musician (if you could call it that), I learned how to be frugal. I was so dedicated to working on my music that I did a lot of jobs that gave me my independence, while at the same time allowed me the opportunity to play in small clubs and work on my act. I taught music lessons, cleaned houses, organized people's garages, worked as a personal assistant, and took many odd jobs just to pay the rent.

One day someone called me and asked if I taught guitar. At the time I didn't know how to play, but my rent was due and I needed money, so I told them, "Sure!" For ten dollars an hour, I would teach them the chords I had learned the night before, and I taught myself how to play in the process.

The beginning of changing my consciousness around money came with a simple subscription to a music magazine. The offer said you could check off whatever box that applied to you, either $30 for a regular subscription or $15 for the "starving musician" subscription. I realized I had defined myself as a starving musician for years. Sure, I was making somewhat of a living as a musician, but I was penny pinching. However, in that moment I saw that if I kept defining myself in that way, that is what would keep showing up for me. I chose to check the "regular subscription" and within months my gigs increased, and so did my income.

I have seen through the years how this abundance consciousness shows up daily in small choices as well as in bigger ones. It is very common that I need to schlepp a lot of bags when I travel, and it has been almost a test to see how often I will "treat" myself to a paid luggage cart or someone to handle my luggage.

A great test of this for me occurred when I was coming home from a cross-country gig. I was facing a marathon day of flying, with two connections and a long layover. When I checked in for my first flight, the ticket agent casually mentioned that there was one more seat left in first class for a discounted price. I stood there at the ticket counter, squirming and struggling with the idea of spending the extra money it would take to buy the upgrade. I went over all the pros and cons: how much I was making for the gig versus how much this seat would cost. I almost felt that the woman behind the counter was my subconscious processing me through all my money issues. She coaxed me on by saying how long a flight it would be, how every seat in economy was filled and I would be much more comfortable in first class.

Throwing all my "reasons" aside, I said yes and started on my adventure. I didn't know I would also be upgraded on the first flight as well and that during my two hour layover I could relax in the first class lounge equipped with all kinds of beverages, TV, Internet, and comfy sofas. By the time I got on the final flight home I was happy and relaxed. Between the free movies, the wonderful dinner and dessert, and my every need being taken care of, I was transformed. I laughed when I thought about the ticket agent saying, "You'll never want to fly any other way again!" When I opened my mail the next day, I was amazed to find an unexpected royalty check for exactly the amount of my upgraded ticket. Seems that Spirit was just waiting for me to say yes to my abundance and affirm it as soon as I made the leap!

"Prosperity is a way of living and thinking, and not just money or things. Poverty is a way of living and thinking, and not just a lack of money or things." — ERIC BUTTERWORTH

Prosperity Chant
Words and Music: Karen Drucker

What do I want? What do I desire?
What will bring me to my highest good?

Prosperity, I claim it. Abundance, it is mine.
Love flows through me. I feel joy all the time.

> CHORUS:
> I can have it. I deserve it. I claim it. It is mine.
> I can have it. I deserve it. I am it. It is mine.

Peace fills my heart. I surrender everything.
Health is my birthright. Passion helps me sing.

> CHORUS

Anything I want. Anything I desire.
Anything that brings me to my highest good.

I release and let go. I accept what is mine.
I can have what I want, and let Spirit direct the flow.
Life is good! Life is fun! Life is great! This song is done!

CHAPTER 5

I've Got the Power

With all the odd jobs I had in my youth, it wasn't until I became a teenager that I learned that the best way to make guaranteed, dependable money was being a babysitter. With my first babysitting job, I realized I could be making money for just watching TV, doing my homework, and basically hanging out. This worked for me! I soon established myself as the resident babysitter of Laurel Canyon. I had a little business of taking care of the children in the canyon, back before all the paranoia about what babysitters could do to your kids. Most moms would meet me, see I was a reasonable, intelligent teenager, and hand over their kids to me.

When I learned there was a new mom moving onto my street, I prepared to go make my presentation and tell her how I would be the best babysitter for her kids, changing their lives forever. I found out that the new mom was singer/songwriter Carole King and that she had two teenage daughters and a one-year-old. I also found out she had a full time nanny who took care of the kids. I marched down to her house anyway, thinking maybe I could be a back up for the nanny. Nervously, I knocked on the door. A kind, older woman named Willamae answered, and I quickly realized that she was the nanny. I certainly didn't want her to think I came gunning for her job. When I nervously gave her my little speech, she threw up her hands and said, "Praise God, now I can have a day off!" We immediately became friends and I became the back up for her on her Sundays off and whenever she was sick.

When I met Carole it was like looking in a mirror. Aside from the fact that she was shorter and fifteen years older than me, we looked like sisters. We immediately bonded, and soon I was spending more time at her house than at mine. Over time, Carole would play the role of older sister/mother and helped to transform the geeky sixteen-year-old that I was. She took me to her hair stylist who cut my hair short and let it go curly, and gave me her hand-me-down muslin shirts and clothes that just spelled HIP. With my hair now short and curly we looked even more similar. I would often be stopped on our street by tourists, thinking they were getting a Carole King sighting and wanting an autograph. Well, of course I complied—what else could I do?

I also did something very radical that no one knows about—up until now. When Carole would get a big envelope from her record company with hundreds of letters from fans, she would look through it for a minute and then, feeling overwhelmed, just throw the whole stack away. Before the trash went out I would always take the time to look through the stack to see if there was a letter from some teenage girl who was just like me, pouring her heart out to Carole, hoping for some kind of connection. I would often write a simple note back thanking them for writing and saying I hoped they would continue to buy my albums. I just couldn't bear the thought of someone feeling not heard or rejected.

I fell in love with Carole's toddler, Molly, and loved spending time with her. I would go there after school every day just to play with her and to take her and Carole's dogs, Schwartz and Lika, for walks in the hills. About a year later Carole was pregnant again, and I was fully in the family. Every Sunday I went over around 8:00 a.m. and took her car down the hill to buy lox and bagels.

We would all spend the day eating, hanging out by her pool, and living the California rock star life. When she bought her house in Malibu, she would have a limo come pick me up for my weekend babysitting duties. When she performed local concerts, the limo would come for me and I would be backstage with Molly and Carole's newborn son, Levi.

I often stayed with her at her beach house in Malibu, and also spent a summer at her house in Canaan, Connecticut. I met her friends James Taylor and Carly Simon, as well as her guru Swami Satchidananda (whom I had the pleasure of watching as he drove a speed boat all around the Santa Barbara Channel with his white beard and robes blowing in the wind). I was babysitting for Carole the night she won her Grammy Awards for her album "Tapestry." We all cheered every time "Mommy's" name would be announced for another category, for which she would win yet another Grammy. I was there when she cried over the problems in her marriage, and I would listen and be a friend. I never even thought until years later what an interesting relationship we had. She would confide in me like a peer, and at sixteen I guess I was there for her in a way that some of her other friends were not. This experience probably explains why I have always had friends who are about ten years older than me.

When Carole was in the process of remodeling her house to build a home recording studio, the upright piano in her old studio had to be moved. I came home one day and found, to my amazement and shock, that her piano was now in my bedroom. She knew I wanted to learn to play and she let me "borrow" her piano until her studio was built. Luckily for me the process took a year. That was a turning point in my life. I would come home every day, write my teenage angst songs, and teach myself how to play the piano. I couldn't sing well and was very self-conscious about it. When I mentioned this to her, she said if you sang your own songs it didn't matter how well you could sing. That was my invitation. I wrote and wrote and eventually started to perform my songs at open mike nights around Hollywood.

It wasn't all idyllic, though. Carole was going through typical mother-daughter issues with her oldest daughter. Louise was a talented singer and songwriter, and was acting out in teenage fashion by rebelling against her mother. I, on the other hand, appeared to be like "Miss Goody Two-Shoes." Since Carole was not my mother, I seemed like the ideal child to her, and she would often introduce me as her oldest daughter. Since we looked so much alike no one ever questioned it.

Around the time of my high school graduation Carole's life with her husband, Charlie, was starting to fail, and she began pulling back from everything that her whole life with Charlie represented, which included me. She sold her house in Laurel Canyon and our bond was broken. She eventually moved to Idaho and I went off to college. I went to see her a few times at concerts, but I was clearly on the outside. Just getting backstage past the security people was an effort, and I felt awkward and shy.

I never really thought about what an amazing situation I had until I went off to college and told my girlfriends about my life in Hollywood. I thought that everyone had experiences like mine. Now I see how divinely blessed I was to have had this opportunity and how the path of my life started with my just knocking on a door one summer afternoon when I was sixteen.

I have not seen Carole since those days, and yet I have dedicated some of my CDs to her. I truly think I wouldn't be doing what I am doing now had it not been for her coming into my life at such a critical time. I believe in divine timing, and my relationship with Carole was the manifestation of it. I can hear the influence she has had in my writing, and I wonder sometimes if she would get a kick out of knowing how she changed my life forever. I have thought about writing to her, but then remember back to those long-ago days when the notes would wind up on a secretary's desk or be thrown out in the trash. But who knows? Maybe there is another teenager working for her who would save my letter from the trash and write back to me.

"I've been absolutely terrified every moment of my life — and I've never let it keep me from doing a single thing." — GEORGIA O'KEEFE

I've Got the Power

Words & Music: Karen Drucker

CHORUS:
　　I've got the power to make all my dreams come true.
　　I've got the power, there's nothing I can't do.
　　I've got the power to be anything I want.
　　I've got the power inside of me.

Everyday I'm wastin' my time thinking,
that someone else is gonna do it all for me.
I've got to get up, get out, get it, just get started.
Take one step towards my destiny.
I'll define my direction with clear cut intention.
Declare what will be and then watch it come to me.

　　CHORUS

There are days when I feel that I'm just no good.
Days when I don't even want to try.
But when I stop, look and listen and surrender,
I hear a voice of truth I cannot deny.
It says "You know you can do it, just get down to it.
Have faith in yourself and the will to see it through."

　　CHORUS

In those times when I feel so frightened
and it seems like I just can't go on.
I've got to look deep inside 'cause that's where
I find the power inside of me!

　　CHORUS

CHAPTER 6

The Call of Something More

Narelle

I never had the illusion that being a singer would be glamorous. If I had, I think I would have been a little bitter. I grew up seeing the life of what being at the pinnacle of your career looked like. In my years of working for Carole King, I would go shopping with her before she went on tour. She would go from store to store buying all the coolest performing clothes. Limos would pick her up for her gigs, and people waited on her to make sure she had everything she needed to perform. But I also saw the hard work it took to "make it."

When I started singing professionally in my early twenties, I knew I would have to be creative to find ways to pay my rent. I began teaching music lessons, singing in hotels, blues-bars, private parties, and doing lots of "odd jobs." For example:

✓ I was a singing mermaid at The Monterey Bay Aquarium, where I was hired to sit on top of the piano in full mermaid attire with my fin flipping while singing fish songs for four hours. After singing songs from *The Little Mermaid* and classic fish songs like "Beyond the Sea" and "How Deep Is the Ocean,"

I found it quite a challenge to fill the time. Also, it was a sight to see when I took breaks and literally had to hop in my fin to the break room.

✓ I was a tap dancing, singing casket for the California Funeral Directors where my comedy partner, Lauren, and I sang rewritten lyrics to "Stand by Your Man," which became, "Stand by Your Urn." They also loved the rewrite to the Linda Ronstadt song, "When Will I Be Loved," with the lyrics changed to "I've been treated, fluid depleted. When will I be embalmed?" Who knew that funeral directors were such a wild and crazy bunch?

✓ I was a "rapping" computer walking around an outdoor expo singing my rap song, performing in 100-degree heat inside a contraption that looked like a giant computer with only my face and arms sticking out. All the Silicon Valley tech people at the party would run when they saw me coming, fearful that I would grab them and make them sing with me onstage.

✓ I have delivered hundreds of singing telegrams. I would burst into an office dressed in some colorful rainbow outfit, with a crazy hat and a toy monkey clanking these two cymbals together, and seek out my recipient. I could usually figure out who it was in a nanosecond by the mortified look and sheer terror in the person's eyes. Their "friends," who were the ones who paid for them to be so embarrassed, were usually doubled over laughing while I sang some clever version of "Happy Birthday" to them. Sometimes this job made me feel as if I were a dentist because the person was always so thrilled when I was done.

✓ I've sung Christmas songs in a moving elevator. Just imagine after a long day at work, just wanting to get home, you press the down button, and when the elevator opens here I am sitting behind an electric piano belting out "Joy to the World!" To say people were not thrilled is a mild understatement. They would immediately press another down button to close the elevator door and get rid of me as fast as they could.

✓ In the "I'll-Sing-Anything-Anywhere-At-Anytime-Department": I was hired to sing at the "dinner" of a computer software company with my starting time to be 4:30 a.m. This was a Hawaiian-theme party for all the workers who worked the all-night late shift. There was a massive spread of Hawaiian delicacies with a giant pig roasting in front of the bandstand. We were hired to play energetic rock and roll as the workers came in for their luau. The combination of hardly any sleep plus the smell of that pig in front of us made some of my band members turn an interesting shade of green. I must admit, though, that it was great to be done with work before the rest of the world was even waking up!

✓ For the twelve days of Christmas, I was hired to wear a full green elf outfit, complete with green turned-up elf shoes, and walk around all the floors of Macy's bursting into Christmas songs, hopefully getting people to sing along. Children would smile at me, adults would give me a pitiful glance, and the gangs of teenage girls would roll their eyes and say in that Valley Girl tone, "Oh my Gawd, look at her, she is like soooooo stupid."

I won't even talk about all the nightclubs I have played where the smell of cigarettes and beer would be so palpable that I swear I would have that smell seeping through my pores. I would air out all my clothes and have to take a shower and wash my hair at 2 a.m. when I came home; otherwise, my sheets would smell like a bar. And dare I forget to mention the blues club that had a chain link fence in front of the stage to spare the musicians from the beer bottles that might be thrown at you if a patron didn't like the song you just selected.

I am a true working musician, and I would have to say I have done it all!

When I first started out actually making a meager living as a musician, I was thrilled. I would play solo piano jobs at hotels in San Francisco where I was probably hired not for my ability to play and sing, but simply because I was female. Since I would work Monday through Friday, ninety-five percent of the people coming into the bar where I worked were traveling businessmen. I was "encouraged" to talk to them— meaning the longer I could keep them there, the more they would drink and the more money the bar would make. I worked at one hotel where the grand piano was made into the actual bar so that people would sit around the piano, drinking and smoking in my face and saying, "Hey little lady, play 'Misty' for me." I would have my little tip jar prominently displayed with the $5 bill that I would stick in there, hoping that by the end of the night there would be more. Some nights I just took home my $5, and on good nights when the bar was filled and everyone was singing along with me, my tip jar would be stuffed to the top.

At that point, though, making my living as a musician meant I was able to give up my day job. I had been doing all kinds of odd jobs just to pay the rent and keep my nights free for playing any open mike night or small cabaret that would have me. I had started a business called "Rent-A-Wife" for all the single businessmen who I knew had no time for cleaning house, grocery shopping, or errands. It was a perfect job for me. I would crank up their expensive stereos, clean their house, and sing away, fantasizing that these beautiful houses with a view of San Francisco were mine. They would leave me a check and I would rarely ever see them. One day one of my clients asked me what I really wanted to do, and when I confessed I wanted to be a musician, he made some calls. The next week I gave up house cleaning and was singing at a fancy hotel in San Francisco.

This was my first steady job singing at a hotel bar right in the heart of the city. It was great—a regular paycheck, security, predictability. I was a full-time working musician and I was thrilled. The bar was called "The Poets Pub," and there were huge black and white drawings of dead poets with creepy stares lining the red velvet walls. The piano was so old and broken down that after playing it all week, my fingers would get sharp pains in them. As for the location, you know you are not in a great area when the winos on the street know you by name!

At first it was a wonderful gig. After about eight months, however, I would find myself getting tired and cranky, and wanting to slap anyone who asked me to sing "Piano Man" for the hundredth time. I would go outside on my breaks and cry, feeling that there must be something more for my life than this. I remember feeling energized during the day, but as I would drive to this job, the feeling of tiredness and apathy would literally creep into my body. It was as if my body knew it was time to make a change before my mind wanted to admit it. A favorite quotation of mine is "Pain pushes until the vision pulls." I have seen how this truth has worked to move me along in my life, especially when I was scared to make a change.

In that pain of not knowing that something (anything!) else could be possible, I started reading any self-help book I could find. I was depressed and stuck, and knew that I needed help. (Little did I know that years later some of the authors I read then would be speaking at some of the conferences where I was hired to sing.) One idea stuck with me: "Act As If." The exercise was to imagine what you wanted so clearly that you could actually feel it happening to you...not later, not any of the usual "well, if (fill in the blank) happens, then I can have it." This was all about seeing what you wanted, feeling it, describing it, and doing whatever actions you needed to do to make it real, right now. This was a brand new concept for me and, since I had nothing to lose, I tried it.

I started fantasizing about where I wanted to perform. Being young and single, and wanting to travel, I decided that working for a cruise line would be perfect for me. I loved Hawaii, so I found out all the information I could about American Hawaii Cruise Lines. They said I would need a thirty-minute show, with arrangements for a seven-piece band, and, of course, a performance wardrobe. I had none of these things, and no idea how to get any of them. The key, though, is that now I had a goal, a lofty one, something to make those long nights at the bar have purpose and meaning. When no one was in the bar, which was usually the first and last hour of the night, I would work on the songs for the show, practice my routines, and keep writing my "Act As If" life plans. When I felt I was ready, I sent a letter and demo tape off to the cruise line and waited..and waited...and waited.

After a few months of calling and not getting any response from the cruise line, I could feel myself slipping back into hopelessness. I kept reading and working on these new principles of dreaming big, but I was getting discouraged.

Just around the time I finally decided it was time to let go of my single focus on that particular cruise line and start looking for other options, an unexpected miracle occurred. It was another boring night at The Poet's Pub—a few businessmen drinking in the corner, the dead poets in the paintings staring down at me, Larry the bartender dozing off behind the bar. All of a sudden a good-looking man came and sat at the piano bar. He requested a few songs and started singing along with me. To my amazement he was a great singer, and I immediately perked up. Just having someone to sing with helped to make the night more tolerable. I sang a set with him, and at the break asked him who he was and why the heck he was in this weird bar. Turns out he was a singer from a cruise ship that was in dry dock in San Francisco. The whole crew was being put up for a week in this hotel while the ship was being worked on. When I casually asked what ship it was, his answer practically knocked me off my barstool. You guessed it—an American Hawaii Cruises ship.

Needless to say, I told him my story, and within a month I had quit my job and was in my sequin dress, doing a thirty-minute show for American Hawaii Cruises with a seven-piece band backing me up. Since I had experience playing piano and singing, I sang in the lounge four nights a week as well. I loved that job, met fabulous people, and to this day I still have friends who were in that band.

The only drawback to this job was if you were singing in a hotel bar and some drunken person was loud and obnoxious, you would probably never have to see him again. But on a cruise ship, you would probably be sharing a breakfast table with him in the morning!

I learned a great lesson from the transition of playing in hotels bars to being on the cruise ship. I really had to "Act As If" to change my circumstances. As Oprah Winfrey says, " Luck is where opportunity and preparation meet." Yes, meeting that singer that night was pure luck, but the fact was that even with no sign that this new opportunity could come along, I just knew there was something more for me than singing in that hotel bar, and I got ready for it. I hired someone to arrange songs for me, bought fancy dresses (on credit since I didn't have the money to pay cash), and planned this imaginary show knowing that someday, one day, it would happen.

I worked on the cruise ships until, once again, the call of something more came and I had to trust there was more for me to explore. That is one reason for writing this book. Doing so just felt like the next step for me. As I sit here in my little room writing this story, I have no idea what will happen with it, if anyone will read it or if it will be "good" or not. I just know that I am being "called" to write, as I was called to do each step of the many twists and turns that my music career has taken me. I have finally realized how important it is to get quiet enough to hear that call, and then to trust enough to take that leap in faith.

"... and then the day came when the risk to remain tight in a bud
was more painful than the risk it took to blossom."
ANAIS NIN

The Call of Something More

Words: Karen Drucker
Music: Karen Drucker & John Hoy

There's been a storm brewing inside of me,
clouds moving around my heart.
Something's changing that I can't see.
I'm stuck in what I know is safe but not yet where I'm supposed to be.

CHORUS:
I feel the call of something more.
I feel the call of something that I've never felt before.
I feel the call of something more.
I feel the call, asking, what am I here for?
What am I here for? What am I here for?

They say that pain pushes 'till the vision pulls.
It feels like my safety nets have fallen down.
I wish I had a map of where to go.
I've got this feeling in my soul that when I get there I will know.

CHORUS:
I feel the call of something more.
I feel the call of something that I've never done before.
I feel the call of something more.
I feel the call, asking, what am I here for?
What am I here for? What am I here for?

I want to make a move right now though I don't know when or how.
When I trust and know the truth, my heart will point the way.
There is more of me to share, so today I do declare,
I will take that step in faith and let my light shine.

CHORUS:
I feel the call of something more.
I feel the call of something that I've never been before.
I feel the call of something more.
I feel the call, asking, what am I here for?
What am I here for? What am I here for?

CHAPTER 7

This or Something Better

I have to admit, I was a very good wedding singer. At receptions, I somehow had a talent of figuring out the exact time that the salad plates would all be down, which meant the band could eat. This also signaled that it would be twenty minutes before the first dance, which meant that if we ate really fast we could get them up dancing, play a good forty-five minute set, cut the cake, throw the bouquet, and then dance 'em 'till they drop before sending the bride and groom home, picking up our check, packing up the P.A. system, and getting out of there exactly on time. All of these calculations would be happening in my mind at the same time that I was singing "Feelings," "Misty," or "New York, New York."

There were a few slips-ups, though. The "bridges," or middle sections, of many songs are so similar that, after the guitar player took a solo, I had been known to come in singing an entirely different song, but which was in the same key. I was always so blessed to work with such great musicians that they would just raise their eyebrows, signaling to me that I had just totally blown it, and continue on like it was some predetermined medley that we had rehearsed.

From the hundreds of weddings I played, I also developed the rare talent to decipher people's song requests: (best said with a Texas drawl) "Hey, do you folks know that song 'Big Wheels'?"—meaning "Proud Mary," or someone coming up to the band stand and saying, "I bet you all play a mean 'Junk Yard Dog' don't cha?"—meaning "Bad Bad Leroy Brown," or my favorite, "Kittens"—meaning "Misty" ("Look at me, I'm as helpless as a kitten up a tree..."). Then there was always someone who would say, "You know that song, it has the word 'Love' in the title?" Oh yeah, no problem, that narrows it down to about a million choices!

My main job, though, was to move the party along making sure the cake was cut, the bouquet was thrown and people danced 'til the final "Yahoo! Celebrate Good Times" was sung. I would deal with everything from nervous brides having meltdowns to nervous party planners trying to control me and every detail of the event. For example, they would say, "You know, it might be good idea if you sang 'Heard It Through the Grapevine'—I hear the kids just love that one." It took everything I had at times not to yell at them about how I really knew what I was doing and to leave me alone! Then there were the clinging mothers of the bride who couldn't bear to see the event end since it had given them such bonding and connection with their daughter. I somehow juggled it all, kept everyone happy, and had my band working every weekend.

As a "singer for hire," I would do just about any kind of gig to pay the rent. I sang at weddings, corporate parties, hot dog stand openings—you name it. I would be there in my little black tuxedo dress, ready to sing anything the client wanted. I eventually developed so much wedding business that I would have to squeeze in as many weddings as I could fit into a weekend. It was common to play an afternoon wedding from 12:00-4:00 p.m, then race to some other location in the Bay Area to do a 6:00-10:00 p.m. gig. The only problem with this was keeping all the couples and their specific song requests straight. I would have so many wedding information sheets on my music stand between my afternoon and evening gigs on the weekends that eventually all of the details would turn into a blur. There were endless lists of songs wanted, people to introduce, members of the family that I would have to look out for ("Whatever you do, DON'T let Uncle Harry take the mike to say ANYTHING!), and, most important, what couple I was singing for. I developed the technique of simply saying, "And now let's welcome our bride and groom to the dance floor for their first dance," only after I made the giant mistake of saying, "Now let's welcome Bob and Tammy," and having the bride I was introducing give me the look of death as she screamed, "NO — IT'S JANET AND JEFF!!!!!!"

Then there were the "agents." Not the agents you think of in the Hollywood sense, who were there to represent you and to help you become a star. Oh no. These were simply "wedding brokers" who would handle all the details from the flowers to the catering to booking the band. If they could sell the nervous bride on letting them handle everything, they could make a fortune by quoting her huge prices for the "best band in town," only to turn around and tell us, "Ya know, there's just not a lot of money on this one. Sorry." We would agree to do the job for a cheaper price, then drive up to the private home which was obviously a million-dollar mansion, and find out that this wedding was about a three hundred thousand dollar event. Yeah, right, "No money."

Or there was the agent who would use my demo tape and all of my promo to sell the client, but not show my picture. Then when I would be on a job that weekend, one of the musicians would come up to me and say, "Hey Karen, you sounded great last night." When I informed him that I hadn't sung the previous night, he would tell me about how the agent sold the client on "The Karen Drucker Band" and had the girl singer say her name was Karen, just so he could make more money on a cheaper band.

I learned many lessons and made many mistakes. Some of my most memorable, and some of my worst experiences were with bar mitzvahs. These gigs were by far the hardest because the party is essentially for the thirteen-year-old boy, but typically the parents spend a fortune wanting the "perfect party" for their son while also wanting to show off to their friends. All night long we would try to please the parents with some nice easy listening standards, but the young boys would stand at the base of the stage looking up at us and sneering. They'd say things like, "You guys suck. Can't you play any (whatever the current 'in' band is)?" I would then switch to something a little more current (which is pathetic, because my idea of current songs stopped at "Pink Cadillac" and "YMCA"), which then led to the parents coming up and yelling at me for playing music that was too loud and raucous. They would then request "Moon River," and we'd go through the whole cycle again.

The main event of the evening, though, is the candle lighting ceremony where the boy lights thirteen candles, with each candle honoring someone in his family. The procedure is that he stands in front of the candle and, while lighting it, says, "And here is a candle for my Aunt Lulu, who came all the way from Kansas City." As he lights the candle, I strike up the band to play eight bars of "Kansas City" while Aunt Lulu runs up to plant a big sloshy kiss on the kid. This goes on a total of thirteen times, with different names and songs attached to each candle.

The bar mitzvah that I will always remember, though, was for Ralphie, a cute kid who was embarrassed to be doing any of this in the first place. However, he knew that if he made it through this part of the evening, he could get to the big payoff of all bar mitzvahs—the opening of his gazillion presents. He went through his list, looking down at the paper, nervously reading the names. I directed the band with the rehearsed songs that were all agreed upon ahead of time. But somehow at the end, Ralphie screwed up. He was supposed to introduce his brother, Ritchie, who was the wild one and a real joker. The parents had picked the old Chuck Berry tune, "Great Balls of Fire," for Ritchie's big moment of running up to the stage. The band was ready to hit the downbeat of the song on my cue. Instead, Ralphie mixed up candle #12 with Candle #13 and said, "And now I'd like to light a candle for all the Holocaust victims." As if the camera was pointed on me in a slow motion freeze frame, I yelled out to the band, "Noooooooo—doooon't plaaaaayyy soooonnngg.

Stoooooopppppp!" Luckily the piano player immediately caught the mistake and just played the most somber thing he could think of in a split second decision.

Somehow we made it through the rest of the night, and somehow I have been able to wean myself away from doing many more bar mitzvahs and weddings!

"The purpose of our lives is to give birth to the best which is within us." — MARIANNE WILLIAMSON

This or Something Better

Words: Karen Drucker
Music: Karen Drucker & John Hoy

CHORUS:
This or something better is waiting for me.
I know that this or something better
is the key that will set my heart free.

I'm gonna let go of control, I'm gonna get out of my way.
I know the Universe conspires to bring me heaven today.

CHORUS

I'm tired of playing it small, of doing what I think I should.
The Universe stands up to meet me,
to claim my highest form of good.

CHORUS

I know it - I claim it - I have it right now!

CHORUS

I'm gonna say yes to my dreams, let my imagination soar.
I know that I have gifts that I must use,
that is what I was put here for.

CHORUS

CHAPTER 8

Taming My Inner Critic

I am about to record the vocal. All the music tracks have been done. The band tracks and back-up vocals sound perfect, and now it's my turn. I feel my stomach getting queasy and my palms starting to sweat as I approach the vocal booth. I put the headphones on, the engineer starts the track, and I start singing. All of a sudden I hear this voice in my head saying, " What are you trying to do? This song is horrible! It isn't funny, it's trite and poorly written and the worst part is that you are singing off key! Mayday, mayday—abandon this nonsense, get out while you can."

I stop the track and start to laugh. I get it. The song I am about to record is called "Taming My Inner Critic" and she is having her way with me. The song is describing what she does to me and how I am taking back my power, and she does not like this idea. She is being found out, busted, being put into the spotlight, and she is not a happy camper. Even though I have learned techniques to help me "tame" her when I am recording a song, like taping up pictures on my music stand of cheering audiences or letters from people saying my songs have helped them through hard times, she can still make her way into my head and try to sabotage any project I do.

Today I can laugh about it but for years she tortured me.

From the first time I auditioned for the Hollywood High School choir in tenth grade, when she got me so worked up that my throat literally closed (I didn't make it into choir), to the times when I tried out for jobs or went on dates, I would get a stream of reasons from my inner critic why I couldn't do it or why it wouldn't go well. I have learned that whenever I was stretching, growing, or changing, she would get on the warpath to change my mind. I finally realized that it was as if she had a job description she followed to the law, to keep me in the same stuck place, no matter what, with no change, no growth, no transformation of any kind...making sure I stayed the same and kept it status quo.

When I finally connected the dots that her voice got louder whenever I tried something new, I actually started to have compassion for her. She was just doing her job. A job, that somehow, some part of me had hired her to do, and what a great job she was doing. Each CD that I made, each show that I performed, any time I would stretch, would cause her to scream, yell and manipulate me to stay safe, secure, and the same. (You should just hear what she is saying—or yelling—right now as I stretch and write this book, especially this chapter!)

But the problem is I am kind of a growth junkie. I love to challenge myself, expand my horizons, and learn new things.

So, Zelda, as I call her, and I sat down and had a heart-to-heart talk. I made a deal with her. When I know something big is coming up, I will acknowledge the good job she has done, tell her how important this new thing is to me, and then invite her to leave for a little while and go have a Caramel Frappuccino at Starbucks—on me! I will pack her a lunch, give her money for a movie, do whatever it takes to have her go away and keep her occupied as I do the new big thing. Even now as I write this, she is hovering over my shoulder comparing what I am writing to the writing of all of my friends who make their livings as writers. Does she completely go away? Can I make the voice just stop?

Can I still go for my dreams with all the constant chattering happening?

For me, I know she is always here, but I don't let her stop me anymore. The main thing I do is focus on the higher purpose of what I am doing. When I am recording a song that just might help someone who is going through cancer treatments, I tell Zelda, "Get out of my way, there's a bigger plan here!" Now when she starts wailing away, I just have a little laugh because I know I must really be stretching and growing, and I let her be, let her say what she needs to say... and then proceed.

A student in one of my workshops came up with this quote: "I know you are there, I hear what you say, but that is simply not my truth today."

Uh, oh! I just reread what I wrote and she is starting in with me. I think I'd better send her off to Starbucks for another Frappuccino and leave her there for a while!

"If you hear a voice within you say 'you cannot paint' then by all means paint, and that voice will be silenced." — VINCENT VAN GOGH

Taming My Inner Critic

Words: Karen Drucker
Music: Karen Drucker & John Hoy

She howls she bites,
she wants to take me down with all of her might.
She snarls she growls, but now I am ready to put up a fight.
I've been in therapy for a hundred years, and there's a peace that I've finally found.
I've let go of so many fears and she is not gonna kick me around.

    CHORUS:
    I'm taming my inner critic.
    You're not welcome here any more.
    I'm taming my inner critic.
    Allow me, to kick you out the door.

She kvetches, she complains, her demands make me feel so insane.
Every detail of my life is analyzed and sliced up with her knife.
But I am woman just watch me roar,
with a force that she can't ignore.
Every positive word I say gives me the power to chase her away.

    CHORUS:
    I'm taming my inner critic.
    You're not gonna win at this game.
    I'm taming my inner critic.
    If this is how you spend your days, you should feel ashamed.

    I'm taming my inner critic.
    From now on I win and you lose.
    I'm taming my inner critic.
    You know the truth? You are like so yesterday's news!

But she says: "You know you're not very smart. Don't even try.
You're gonna fail."
And I say: "I am enough!"
But she says: "You shouldn't eat that donut.
Are you gaining weight?
Is that another wrinkle?"
And I say: "I am beautiful!"
But she says: "You know you're not really that good, or talented.
Why don't you just play it safe?" "
And I say: "I am worthy!"
I say: "Get off. Get back. It's now. It's time to claim
this life as mine!"

CHORUS:
I am taming my inner critic.
You have no power over me.
I'm taming my inner critic.
Knowing my worth has finally set me free!
So back off!

CHAPTER 9

I Don't Have to Be Perfect

B ecause I grew up in Hollywood, I know firsthand about illusions. I have been on the backlots of studios that were made to look like Anytown, USA. Or the backlot would look like a western town where cowboys rode in for the big showdown, but I knew it was just a set-front in smoggy Burbank, California. There would be a bunch of extras hanging around, drinking their lattes in period costumes, talking on cell phones, and listening to their iPods until it was time to be called back to the set.

I have also known enough celebrities to see that there is the public persona and the personal one. I have always been amazed at how different some celebrities are from the way they are seen by the world. It's really their publicist who should get the Academy Award for helping them to uphold that false image.

I have seen in my own life how people get ideas about how things are and think that is the way it really is. For example, some people have an idealized image of what a songwriter's life is like. I have had people tell me they have this image of me sitting every morning at a grand piano, with a steaming cup of coffee next to me, singing and playing and creating magical songs that will inspire and heal the world. Of course, this is after an hour of meditation and yoga in which I first commune with God, have all my chakras opened and cleaned, and am ready to receive the gifts of creativity that will trickle down from the Universe.

Actually as I write this, I am in a little corner of the Dallas/ Fort Worth airport with a two-hour layover to take me to my gig in North Carolina this weekend. I will probably spend the time writing a song. I have written songs on airplanes, in taxis, when

I walk, when I am shampooing my hair (not a very convenient time to have a song appear), and in just about every kind of situation. I even had a full song "download" in my head ("I'll Light a Candle") while I was swimming my "laps" in the San Francisco Bay about a half-mile from shore. I wanted so badly to remember the song, that I sprinted into the shore. I found a tourist walking along, looking out on the Bay with a cell phone in his hand, and asked if I could make a quick call. Appearing stunned, he handed over his phone. I called into my answering machine, sang the chorus of the song before I could forget it, thanked him, and jumped back into the water to finish my swim. I remember the bewildered tourist walking away mumbling, "These people in San Francisco really are nuts!"

So in other words, creativity can happen whenever, however, anytime, anywhere, and I just have to be willing to be open, and have a pen, paper or tape recorder handy. But the main thing I have found about creativity of any kind is:

I have to be willing to not be perfect.

Oh that word. Perfect. That unrealistic-set-the-bar-so-high-that-no-one-can-achieve-it word. There's that idea we can't do something until we're "perfect." I realized that if I waited until I thought I was perfect at songwriting, singing, performing, or whatever, I would still be waiting on the sidelines. When I was a wedding singer years ago, I remember going to a bookstore to look at the wedding section. I was amazed to see the word "perfect" in just about every title: *Your Perfect Wedding, Your Perfect Day, How to Have Everything Be Perfect on Your Special Day.* Talk about a set up! No wonder the brides who hired my band were stressed and emotional—the pressure of perfection was almost too much to bear.

When I write a song, not only do I have to tell my critic to take a back seat, but I have to allow and surrender to the process of having whatever comes out be whatever it is. Sloppy, disorganized, rambling—whatever. Sometimes it's good, sometimes it's horrible, and sometimes there is just a kernel of an idea that could be developed into something else. The main thing, though, is to just let it out, let it be dumped on the page, no matter what form it is in. It's in that time when that judgmental part or "perfect" idea needs to be put aside so the creative part has all the room to express. When I look back on the pages and pages of what started as a song idea, and where it finally got to before I recorded it, it is a fascinating journey. But none of it would have gotten anywhere if I had the umbrella of perfection hanging over me. I have to be able to write a line, scratch it out, and try another one. I have to be able to sing a note, have it be flat or sharp, and keep refining it until it is where I want it to be. I have to be willing to let it be bad and not have any judgment about whatever is coming out. If anyone saw or heard me in this vulnerable infant stage and gave me an opinion or negative comment, it would shut that creative process down. The only time I finally stop changing and rewriting is when I go into the recording studio to record my lead vocal. That's when I have to allow it to be whatever it is and let it go and let it have a life of its own.

I received an email from a singer recently whom I had worked with at a retreat. She asked: "Can I really sing? I want to sing so badly! I want to be good but I'm so afraid. I have this critical voice in my head that tells me people are just trying to make me feel good, that maybe I am fooling myself. What should I do?"

And here is how I replied:

Dear Sue,

I have made my living as a singer for about thirty years and there are days when I still don't know if I am any good.

It's a daily spiritual practice to get out of your way, out of your head, and just keep trying to get better and to learn and grow and fall down, and think you are horrible, and then try again, and then take it in when people say you are good, and then doubt them, and then have moments where maybe, just maybe, you might not really be as horrible as you thought, and then sometimes feel like you are good, and then two days later doubt yourself, and then you do a performance where you even impress yourself, and then you worry that you are getting a big head, and then the next night you sing again and this time you say to yourself, "What were you thinking? You really are horrible," and then someone comes up to you on your break and says with tears in their eyes that the song you sang really moved them, and then you think, "What a jerk I am. I have been given this opportunity to share my gift. Who am I to doubt it and slap Spirit in the face?" and then you get all humbled and vow to keep going, and it goes on and on and on and on....

So in other words, take lessons, sing for free, sing for pay, sing at talent shows, sing at convalescent homes, sing, sing, sing, and just keep allowing your heart to open and express. Who knows what it will lead to. And you know what? It doesn't matter what anyone else thinks. It's what you think and how you feel when you are doing it. There is a Swedish proverb that says: "Those who wish to sing always find a song." So find your song — and sing it!

The other part of perfection has to do with society's views of how we are supposed to be. When we see a perfect-looking woman in a magazine, most of the time the photo has been airbrushed even after the woman has been worked on for hours by stylists and makeup people. One of my favorite quotes is from the supermodel Cindy Crawford who said, " Even I don't look like Cindy Crawford in the morning." The same is true for singers in the recording studio. By the time you hear an album or a song on the radio, many times if there was any note that was not right, it simply was "auto-tuned" so that every note is "perfect." A computer program can simply take the note that was sharp or flat and correct it. It's interesting to imagine how many famous singers have made a career being dependent on sound engineers to make them appear perfect when they really couldn't sing well at all.

I love the creative process, and I love helping people find their own outlets for whatever wants to be expressed. I feel that we all have unique gifts to share, but we have to work with our inner critics and take away the idea that we have to be perfect.

One of my favorite quotes is from Adam Osborne who said, "The most valuable thing you can make is a mistake — you can't learn anything from being perfect." So let's celebrate our mistakes, our uniqueness, and the fact that we're not perfect!

"You have been taught that there is something wrong with you and
that you are imperfect, but there isn't and you're not."
CHERI HUBER

I Don't Have to Be Perfect

Words & Music: Karen Drucker

CHORUS:
I don't have to be perfect.
I'm doing the best I can.
I give myself permission to be just who I am.

It started in third grade, the teacher said
"Let's sing and have some fun."
So I let it rip and let it wail and she said
"Karen why don't you just hum?"
So for many years I squished my voice always thinking I was
wrong,
until one day I learned the truth and now I sing this song that
says...

CHORUS

I'm standing in front of the mirror obsessing about my belly fat.
My thighs, my butt, wrinkles 'round my eyes, who can live with
judgment like that?
The media tells me daily I should be young tall tan and thin.
But the truth is when I accept myself, that's when I win! I say...

CHORUS

BRIDGE:
Perfection's an illusion. I won't give my power away.
I can lighten up and let it go and know that I'm OK.

Now I'm older and wiser and I don't really care what people say.
If someone thinks I'm not perfect,
well I just bless them on their way.
Life's too short to be judgmental, take a break, have a good time.
If you're struggling with this issue, just raise your voice with mine
and sing...

CHORUS:
I don't have to be perfect.
I'm doing the best I can.
I give myself permission to be just who I am.

CHAPTER 10

One Small Step

As a musician who plays private parties, I was always busiest during the month of December. Normally I was booked for law office parties, end of the year celebration parties, company parties— you name it. I would be there with my merry band year after year doing hip jazz arrangements of "Frosty the Snowman," "Jingle Bells" and "White Christmas." December was a time when we would work every job we could get because January's calendar was always bare.

One memorable December day I had sung at 7:30 a.m. for a company breakfast, played a children's Santa's tea party for lunch, did cocktails for one company at 5:30 p.m., then raced down the street to join my band at a law office party starting at 8:00 p.m. I would usually work so hard that by the time Christmas day finally arrived, the thought of singing one more "Joy to the World" made me ill. And by that point I usually was ill with a cold or the flu from pushing myself so hard, but I would have the entire month of January to recover since all of the work had dried up.

This particular year was 2001, and it was the first Christmas season in fifteen years I didn't have a gig every weekend singing at a private party. It was less than three months after the attack on the World Trade Center on 9/11, and my band had been booked for every weekend in December until all of my clients started canceling. One by one they called, saying they felt it would be inappropriate to have a party given the trauma that our country was still feeling. What could I say? They had given me enough notice that I was obligated to return their deposits. I was down to one last big party on the first weekend of December and was praying they wouldn't cancel. But, sure enough, I got the call and I had to phone my band members and take them off the job. We cried on each other's shoulders, wondering how we were all going to get by with no work in what was usually the most profitable time of the year.

There I was, a week before that first big weekend in December and I had no work. Nothing. Nada. With all this newfound spare time on my hands, I decided to catch up on some reading. I had just gotten a great book called *Inner Peace for Busy People* by Joan Borysenko. I guess I was meant to read this book, since it practically fell off the shelf at my feet in the bookstore. During this season of peace on earth, I certainly needed some inner peace for myself.

I loved Joan's writing style and was amazed that so many of her stories had the same messages as those in many of my songs. I felt an immediate connection to her and wondered if I should send her some of my music. I looked at her web site and found that she was doing a woman's retreat in Arizona with two other presenters, whom I happened to be friends with. The date of the retreat? The first weekend in December. I called one of the presenters and casually inquired if they had anyone doing music for the weekend. She gave me the retreat organizer's phone number, and just for fun I gave her a call.

When I called and mentioned that I did music for various women's retreats, the woman practically shrieked. It turns out that moments before my call, she had realized they had no one leading the women in singing and drumming. They were filming the retreat for a PBS show called "Women of Power," and the retreat center had provided them with male song leaders. She said she had no more money in her budget, but if I could get myself there I would get the retreat for free, along with room and board.

When I figured out the costs for airfare and for renting a sound system and a keyboard, I immediately thought I couldn't afford it—case closed! I mean spending that money was a ridiculous idea, given the fact I was already losing money by not doing any private parties in December. I was broke! But for some reason the thought of the retreat wouldn't let me go, and my intuition was pulsing through my veins telling me to go. Finally my dear husband simply cut to the core of my agony and said, "You are nuts if you don't go for it." With all of my logic screaming at me not to do this wild, un-guaranteed adventure, I finally trusted my intuition and made the decision to go.

The retreat was amazing, the women were inspiring, and my life was forever changed. Since so many people were still scared to fly after 9/11, what would have been over 150 women at this retreat was now only twenty. This gave us all an opportunity to form a tight bond, and it especially gave Joan and me the chance to connect deeply. Just as I had felt from her writing, she was like a long lost girlfriend/sister, and we started a friendship that weekend that has changed my life. We have worked together at conferences and retreats throughout the years and have always had a wonderful time, but it is our personal relationship that I truly treasure. I realize that taking that one small step, that risk of trusting my intuition, had planted the seed that there was more for me to do than just sing at weddings and private parties.

The weekend was magical for me because it felt like I was at a crossroads between making my living as a wedding singer or going for my dream of singing my own songs. I remember one balmy night at the retreat I went outside under the full moon and stood with my arms outstretched, head lifted back, and just declared: "Ok, Great Spirit, whatever I am supposed to do next, whatever path I am supposed to follow now, I am ready, I am willing, and I am listening." A lone coyote was howling at the moon in the distance and I felt like everything that I knew, everything that was safe and secure, was falling away to make way for something brand-new to come in. All I needed to do was to take that first, small step.

"A journey of a thousand miles begins with one small step."
CHINESE PROVERB

One Small Step
Words & Music: Karen Drucker

CHORUS
One small step, instead of looking at the mountain.
One small step, gets me closer to my goal.
One small step, instead of looking at the mountain.
Then it won't seem like I've got so far to go.

I've got dreams filled with passion.
I've got fears that seem to pop up in my way.
But I've got power that's deep inside my soul.
When I look too far and lose my way,
it always lets me know, that I've gotta take...

CHORUS

I got off the track, I couldn't find my way back.
When I looked inside the truth there could not be denied.
I was making it harder than it had to be,
just pushin' and fightin' until I found the key, that I've gotta take...

CHORUS

CHAPTER 11

I Lost the Right to Sing the Blues

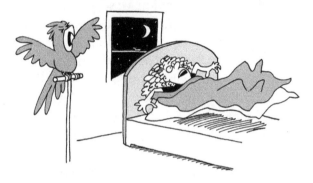

It started with a squeak over in the far right corner. Another quickly followed in the front on the left, then there was one in the middle of the room. Pretty soon little squeaks were happening all over, like fireflies lighting up and squeaking. The problem was that these were not fireflies, and it was a sound I was getting used to every Sunday morning at 10:00 a.m. I was the music director for a New Thought church in Napa, California, and the squeaks were the sound of the elderly congregation turning off their hearing aides as I got up to sing. I had become the music director after substituting at this church for my friend Melissa. When she moved on to another church, I was hired for the job, and now I got to deal with the Sunday morning squeaks.

When Melissa called and asked me to sing for her at this church, I thought she was nuts. What did I know of singing in church? I wasn't religious, and certainly had no idea what New Thought philosophy was all about. However, she convinced me with the idea that I could make a hundred bucks just singing a few "happy songs." Besides, what else would I be doing on a Sunday morning? At the time I was mainly playing weddings or at blues and rock clubs where most of the clientele was either drunk or stoned or throwing things at the band. In comparison, this sounded like a piece of cake.

The congregation was led by an elderly female minister who wanted me to sing opera and show tunes. I did my best, but clearly neither she nor the congregation was thrilled with my weekly selections, which is why the hearing aides were being turned off. The sound system consisted of one knob on the back wall that was controlled by a man who clearly took his job of "sound man" seriously. He decided that whenever I sang with a little too much gusto, he would simply turn the knob just a pinch, which shut my microphone completely off. I would be in the middle of a song and then, poof, I couldn't hear myself at all because the sound system was now turned off.

For some reason I stayed with this job, mainly because I was starting my weekly practice of writing a new song to match the minister's message. After the first few months of going through as many well-known "happy songs" as I could find, I ran out of material and began writing my own. I was getting stimulated, and began resonating with the messages I would hear every week. I had left the blues bars behind and was loving my new life.

Eventually the older minister retired, and so did the show tunes that I still tried to sing for the congregation. A new young, hip minister was hired who wanted Aretha Franklin and Beatles tunes. It was a better match for me for sure, and I stayed until another church in the area asked me to be their music director for better money and a much younger crowd.

I was a church music director for about ten years, and music director for regional and national conferences for another five years. I loved meeting and creating music with talented New Thought musicians. It was exciting to be in charge of the musical events that were located all around the conference sites and scheduled at different times. The work was exhausting but it was also challenging and fun—except when I had to deal with the egos of a few musicians who felt that the world revolved around them and that they should be allowed to "share their gift"—even if "their gift" was singing off key!

When I finally left the security of my church job and took off down the yellow brick road to become a traveling musician, I was petrified. How could I give up a weekly paycheck and people who know me to travel to strange cities, pay my way, stay in strangers' homes, and sing to a different audience every week? How could I not? I had a few CDs out at this point, and it was time to venture out and see if anyone other than my friends would like my music.

The first church I played was huge, with around six hundred people per service. The stage manager told me that I had exactly three minutes to sing my song. I couldn't say anything before my song because they were on a strict timetable. Their services were like a finely tuned machine, and I was just one cog in the wheel. That day I made in CD sales what I would have made in a month of playing my old church. The Universe had given me the sign that I was going to be taken care of, and this was the right next step.

The bands I played with would vary from church to church. Some were top-notch professional musicians who would just read my music charts one time through and be ready to play. Others would range from the classical pianist who would make my rock songs sound like sonatas, to the band who couldn't read music very well. Each instrument would be in different sections of the song with me charging through, trying to get us all to the end. My favorite was an amateur polka band that loved playing at church on Sundays. Needless to say, my gospel song wound up sounding like the "Beer Barrel Polka." Seeing that the train was going in this direction, I had no other choice but to jump on and do-si-do around my lyrics.

Then there are the different technical situations that come with each event. I was doing a sound check before church one time, singing with my CD tracks. I asked the sound man to turn the volume up a bit, but got no response. I asked again, no response. Finally someone came over to me and said, "Karen, that's Fred, our sound man. He's deaf, so he can't hear you." When

I asked about the logic of giving someone who was deaf the job of overseeing the sound, they just said, "Oh, he likes to play with the knobs so much that we can't bear to fire him."

At the beginning of my traveling church life, I would stay at host houses of people in the congregation who would have me as their guest for playing at the church. They were all very kind and warm to me, and I was grateful for a meal and a place to stay. However, the problem was that I wouldn't always know what I was getting. There was the family who put me in the guest room with a divider blocking my view of half the room. I thought nothing of it until at 2:00 a.m., in pitch blackness, this shriek of death bellows from the other half of the room. I woke up with my heart beating, thinking I was being attacked. I find out it's only "Herman," the family parrot, who "just likes to let everyone know he's awake" in the middle of the night. They thought nothing of it, but I never went back to sleep for fear of Herman letting one rip again.

It has been an interesting road and I am forever learning, growing, and evolving to whatever is next along this path. I started out singing blues songs but eventually I learned that I had a whole new song to sing.

"The purpose of life is to be happy." — THE DALAI LAMA

I Lost the Right to Sing the Blues

Words: Karen Drucker & Rita Abrams
Music: Karen Drucker & John Hoy

I woke up this mornin' and somethin' was not right.
My poor head was a-throbbin' 'cause I tossed and turned all night.
This unfamiliar feelin' it shook me up inside.
The truth it was revealin' that a part of me had died.
So I called my higher self and she gave me the bad news.
She said "Your life is just too good,
You lost the right to sing the blues!"

That broken down old Chevy that was eatin' me alive,
I visualized a Lexus and now it's sittin' in my drive.
And that man of mine, that scoundrel, that rotten low down bum,
I've transformed him into a love-God with a sizeable trust fund.
Everywhere I looked I was confronted with the clues,
my life was just so good, I lost the right to sing the blues.

> You can sing the blues if you can't pay the rent.
> You can sing the blues if your money's all been spent.
> But how can I sing the blues, I ain't got no excuse,
> when I'm driving in my Porsche on the way to my masseuse.

So you won't find me wailing late at night in some smoky bar.
And you won't see me cryin' tears into my old guitar.
I'm too busy cleaning my chakras and chasing bad karma away,
and fluffing up my aura, well that could take all day!
Now that I'm enlightened, I gotta spread the news,
when life gets this darn good you've lost the right to sing the blues.

You can sing the blues when your best friend puts you down.
You can sing the blues if your man has done left town.
But what gives me the right to sing that mournful tune,
when I'm steamin' with my honey in my sauna in Cancun!

So now you've heard my story and you understand the pain,
of searching and not finding any reason to complain.
'Cause my stars are in alignment, my house is all feng shui-ed,
I'm filled with peace and harmony, and my bills have all been paid.
I've let go of the struggle, you know I've paid my dues.
When life gets this darn good,
You've lost the right to sing the blues.

CHAPTER 12

Relax, Let Go

I rushed down the stairs through the hoards of people who were coming into the main auditorium to hear the big-name author speak. I was booked at this conference to sing throughout the weekend as an "opening act" for the keynote speakers and to play music in the workshops for the other presenters. Each night I would come down to the main hall that seated about 1,600 people to find out if I was supposed to be up on stage before the speaker started and entertain the people who were there early, ready to be enlightened.

I call this kind of entertaining "Freeway Singing," because it felt like I was standing in the middle of a freeway with this cacophony of noise, trying to sing while people were calling out their friends' names, trying to find each other. To get through it, I just kept repeating the mantra, "Be in service, be in service." I had to leave my ego at the door, as well as any hopes of feeling fulfilled.

Some of the authors were glad to have me sing before they started. They understood that I was creating a tone and energy that would prepare the audience for their talk. Other authors refused to have me sing before them because they thought that having music would be distracting or they just didn't know who the heck I was. Each night I would show up and check in with the stage manager, and would usually be told, "No, they don't want you tonight." In that case, I would allow myself to settle back down, knowing I didn't have to get my adrenaline pumping to entertain and attempt to engage that large crowd. However, when an author would actually feature me as part of their program, it would be an amazing experience. The energy of that large crowd was like driving a Ferrari.

On this particular night, I showed up and again was told I was not needed. Putting my ego and my disappointment in my pocket, I moved to the back of the room and stood there waiting for the famous author to come on. I said my favorite phrase to myself, "It will be revealed." I knew there was a reason I didn't get to sing that night, and if I could just let go, the reason would be revealed.

All of a sudden a woman was standing in front of me. She connected with me at such a deep level that the chaos of people trying to find their seats and bumping into us just vanished. It was as if we were instantly in a bubble. She took my hands in hers and told me that three weeks ago her beloved sister had died of cancer and that she had used my music to help ease her sister through her transition. She said that the closeness they shared, with my music as a backdrop, had been a source of peace and bonding for both of them. I was deeply touched, and we both stood there crying and hugging. She then thanked me and disappeared into the crowd. I never saw her again all weekend

In that moment I got it. In this whole weekend of running from room to room, performing for these authors, selling my CDs, networking, and doing all the schmoozing that goes on at these conferences, this encounter was the real reason I was at this conference.

Before any performance that I do, I always ask Spirit for a sign to show me why I am there. This woman was my sign. She touched me deeply. But more than that, I realized that if I were up on stage performing, as my ego had wanted me to do, I would not have had this sweet moment. Once again it was proven to me that Spirit knows what it's doing. All I need to do is get out of the way and let it be revealed.

"To let go is to fear less and love more." — KAIROS

Relax, Let Go

Words: Karen Drucker
Music: Karen Drucker & John Hoy

CHORUS:
I relax. Let go. Release and surrender.
I relax. Let go. Release and surrender.
I relax. Let go. Release and surrender.
All is well. All is well.

Every day, I affirm and pray,
how I'm blessed with everything I have.
I release my fear 'cause it's all so clear,
I am held. I am loved. I am safe.

CHORUS

Now I see what my life can be,
when I trust in the process and have faith.
And now I know when I just let go,
that I have all I'll ever need.

CHORUS

CHAPTER 13

I Allow, I Surrender

MY WAY

PRISCILLA'S WAY

I learned another great life lesson today: Never believe it 'till you see it, and you just never know....

I had been invited by my good friend, Reverend David Leonard, to do a weekend retreat and concert at his church in Alabama. After being spiritually fed, filled up, and inspired by our wonderful weekend, I was ready for the long trip back home to San Francisco. I arrived at the Huntsville airport about an hour and a half before my flight was supposed to leave. I checked in for my flight at the lovely, uncrowded airport, only to be told that my flight was delayed and that I would probably miss my connecting flight in Dallas. This would result in my getting home at midnight instead of the 8 p.m. time that I had planned.

I immediately felt a wave of tiredness set in. All of my years of doing triathlons and marathons did not help with what looked like a tiring ten-hour ordeal to get home. I groaned and went to my gate for the long wait.

There I proceeded to do what any good spiritual person would do. After my initial "poor me," and "how am I gonna make it through this day??!!" I decided to pray. Why not? What did

I have to lose? I affirmed that I would have energy, and asked for a miracle of any kind (but most specifically, that it would be really nice if the plane actually came in on time!). I also asked to have the patience and ability to let go of my need to control this situation and just to be able to go with the flow. After the prayer I felt better and started reading my book.

Out of the corner of my eye, I saw a shaft of light beaming. I looked up and noticed that across from my gate, in the far corner next to the window, the sun was reflecting on something. Could I be seeing what I thought I was seeing? A beautiful white baby grand piano with the lid up, facing a corner next to Gate 4 in the Huntsville airport? Why would this be? How could this be? I went over to explore and, sure enough, here was a beautiful white Steinway baby grand just shoved in the corner! After looking around to see if there were any alarms that would go off or signs saying "Don't Even Think About Playing This Piano!" I did what any good songwriter with three hours to kill would do. I sat down and started writing songs.

After a while a young policeman named Steven, who worked for the airport, approached me. I thought he was going to bust me and tell me to stop. Instead, Steven told me he was an aspiring musician and asked if he could show me some new songs he had just written. Sitting down and giving me a full-out concert, he asked for my feedback. We had quite a discussion on the pros and cons of a career in music versus the "normal" career that his parents wanted for him.

In that moment, I got how miracles can show up in many forms and how surrendering into the moment opens a path for new possibilities. Steven and I parted as friends, I had written a few new songs, and believe it or not my plane actually arrived on time.

Another lesson in learning to surrender came from my new best friend, Priscilla.

Hers is one of the few voices in my life that speaks to me with complete non-judgment. I can make a mistake, do the stupidest thing, but she never stands there in judgment, crossing her arms over her chest with that look on her face that says, "I can't believe it! I just told you three minutes ago how to do this and here you are, you idiot, doing it wrong again! How many times do I have to tell you?!" No, she doesn't do any of that. She never makes me feel bad about myself. She just repeats one thing every time I make a mistake: "Recalculating."

Priscilla, my new best friend, is my GPS device.

I bought her to help me navigate my way to gigs in some of the unfamiliar cities where I find myself every month. The turning point for me in recognizing the value of a GPS was an experience I had while trying to get to a church in Oregon. I was scheduled to be the guest artist for the day and I had a 7:30 a.m. rehearsal with the band. I got up in plenty of time, had my coffee, and was off, map in hand, with directions given to me by the church. At some point, though, the left turn must have been a right, because I wound up in a field with a bunch of cows. Panicking, I called the church and got their answering machine. I must have prayed really well because from out of nowhere a Highway Patrol car appeared. The officer stopped and gave me directions, whereupon I promptly got lost again, but through some kind of miracle got to the church with a minute to spare.

I ran out to Costco that next week and bought the GPS. My husband programmed the computerized voice with an Australian accent, and I named her Priscilla.

The thing I love about Priscilla is that she is such a great metaphor for life. First of all, you have to know where you are (a good place in life to start). Next you have to know where you want to go (which is another great life idea. How often have I gone from one thing to the next without figuring out where I really wanted to go?). The final step is hooking up to the satellite (like connecting with Source, or Spirit) Then I hit "Go," and Priscilla is off and running, telling me to turn left in 300 feet, make a right at the next ramp, and merge onto the freeway in one mile. The great thing about her, though, is that if I go off course for any reason, she simply, non-judgmentally, in the same tone of voice says, "Recalculating," and gives me new directions incorporating my "mistake." Now instead of feeling discouraged when I make a "mistake," I look forward to hearing her say that word in her Australian accent.

The key to this whole experience is a simple and profound word: surrender. I have to surrender to Priscilla. I have to trust that she knows how to get me to my destination and that I can let go and she will take me there. Every time I don't trust her, every time I refer to my Google maps (backups, in case she lets me down!) and defy her, she keeps recalculating. Yes, I do eventually get to where I want to go but I have fought her the whole way. I think of how often I am stuck in my own need to control, to do it my way, instead of trusting that there could maybe, just maybe, be an easier and gentler way to do something.

I have used this analogy a lot in my life. Every time it seems I am "going off course" and I beat myself up for "making a mistake," I have to remember that this could be Spirit's way of leading me to my highest good. What would my life be like if I were to really surrender, trust, and live with the idea that everything—I mean everything—is perfect? What would my life be like if, instead of thinking I was stupid or criticizing myself, I simply said, "Recalculating" (especially in a soft Australian accent)? What would it look like if my entire life were simply a process of trying something and recalculating, then doing something else and recalculating? What would life be like if it were lived just trusting, surrendering, exploring, having adventures, learning, growing, and lightening up about everything? I tend to think there would be room for a whole lot more joy. And, who knows, another miracle—like Steven, who lifted my spirits that day in the airport—might be just around the corner.

So excuse me, I have to go recalculate.

"If you surrender completely to the moments as they pass, you live more richly those moments." — ANNE MORROW LINDBERGH

I Allow, I Surrender

Words and Music: Karen Drucker

INSPIRED BY
REVEREND DAVID AULT

1st voice: I allow. I surrender.

2nd voice: I receive. I let go. I release. I know.

3rd voice: Love. Joy. Peace.

CHAPTER 14

The Face of God

It was about 2:00 a.m. when I got home. I had just come from a four-hour gig playing to an entire audience of Hell's Angels. It turned out the agent had forgotten to tell me one little detail about tonight's wedding, and that was that the wedding couple were avid bikers and had invited about 150 of their closest leather-clad biker friends to celebrate their nuptials. As a result, instead of the usual two hours of background cocktail music (easy listening and easy to sing), this gig turned out to be four hours of screaming rock 'n roll right out of the gate.

By the end of the night I felt as if I had run a marathon and done a thousand sit ups. Everything in my body hurt, including my brain. So by the time I got home all I could think about was sleep. When I saw the message machine light flashing on my phone however, I made the mistake of listening to the message. It was from the minister of the church where I was the music director.

"Hi love, it's Karyl. Listen, I know it might be a little late notice, but I am doing a talk tomorrow morning about seeing the face of God in everyone you meet. Could you write a little song or chant for me? I've emailed you a few lyric ideas. Thanks!" Click. To say that I was not a happy camper is a mild understatement. I swore, I screamed. I couldn't deal with it. I knew I couldn't do anything right then, so I just went to bed cursing as my head hit the pillow about how I couldn't do anything by tomorrow.

The next morning after five hours of sleep, coffee mug in hand, I sat down at the piano and waited for divine intervention. I had about ten minutes to come up with something brilliant and life-changing around her topic. I took a gulp of coffee and prayed that something would come to me. "Keep it simple" is my mantra when writing chants. If I can have a five-year-old immediately sing it back to me, I know I have done my job. With the few lyric ideas she gave me and some scribbles I had made, I hit a chord and started stumbling around for a melody. I knew that if I allowed myself to get in the way, to listen to that critical inner voice insisting it has to be perfect, or hip, or wondering what people would think about it, nothing would come. This had to be a direct download from Spirit. I guess it worked because in about five minutes a basic form was there, and I raced out the door to make it to church on time.

I worked with Reverend Karyl for many years. We have written many wonderful chants together, and my favorite moments were when I would show her a new song or chant right before the service. Forgetting about the process it took to finish this particular chant she had wanted, I began playing the opening lines, "You are the face of God. I hold you in my heart." Immediately tears sprang to her eyes, and she said it was perfect. I knew it would be sweet when we wove her prayer around this new chant. We sang it that morning, and sure enough, as she asked the congregation to think about different people in their lives, tears were streaming down every face as the congregation sang the chant.

I have often used my songs as my own daily spiritual practice. I try to see the face of God in everyone I meet, including the people who might push my buttons. I notice it's easy with people I love. However, when it's the person who cuts in front of me in line at the store, the grocery checker who might be rude, or the person in the car who practically slams into me while changing lanes, that's when I need to sing this chant.

I have also noticed how much we long to have a connection with each other. When I facilitate workshops, I ask people to walk around the room and sing the chant while taking the time to see the face of God in each other. No matter how many times I do this, I am always amazed at the results. Some people melt and dissolve into a puddle of tears; others can't look people in the eyes or handle the unconditional love coming to them. In my concerts, I have included using sign language when singing this chant. It is really beautiful to see an entire audience signing and singing "You are the face of God" to each other and making a connection.

I guess that is what it is all about for me—connection. With every show or retreat I do, I always pray for the same thing: feeling a connection with people. As simple as this little chant is, I am so inspired to hear about how it has been a bridge for people to connect. There was the story a hospice chaplain told me of a grandfather making his transition, and the whole family, including the grandkids, came into the room and signed and sang this chant to him in his final hours. And there was the couple who sang it for their wedding vows; the woman who sang it as her beloved pet was dying; the youth group from United Centers for Spiritual Living signing and singing to a tribe of children in South Africa, and those children learning it and singing it back to them.

Little did Karyl and I know what a powerful tool for connecting so many people this simple chant would become. Thank God that music offers a tool we all can use to express what is in our hearts to say but what words don't always convey.

"The soul can split the sky in two and let the face of God shine through." — EDNA ST. VINCENT MILLAY

The Face of God

Words by: Karen Drucker & Reverend Karyl Huntley
Music by: Karen Drucker

You are the face of God.
I hold you in my heart.
You are a part of me.
You are the face of God.

(Optional verse):

You are the face of love.
I hold you in my heart.
You are my family.
You are the face of love.

CHAPTER 15

No Is My New Yes

Sometimes you have to be really careful with what words leave your lips.

For a while now I had been saying, "Oh, I just say 'yes' like it's a knee jerk reaction," or "I feel like I am running so fast to catch up with this train, and my legs just can't move that fast."

I had been asked to be the music director for a spiritual conference where, if I accepted the job, I would be responsible for producing and scheduling music from morning 'till night for three weeks straight. I would be overseeing many musicians and performing for thousands of people, so, of course, I immediately said yes. What I forgot to put into the equation were the facts that I was producing another album, preparing my taxes, doing my job as music director for a church, dealing with my mother selling our family home in Hollywood and helping her to move across the country to Wisconsin, as well as handling all of the general day-to-day things that are part of my life. I was also about to leave for a weekend to do three concerts in Arizona and didn't have time to think about anything else. In a "knee jerk" reaction, I just said "yes."

On the Thursday before leaving for Arizona, I was coming out of the shower and put my wet foot down on the freshly waxed bathroom floor. My leg went one way, my body went another, and in one extremely brief moment I had dislocated my kneecap. I shrieked in pain and horror at seeing my completely disfigured knee, and my alarmed husband came running in thinking I was being attacked. It felt like I was being attacked—by my own body! I remember that he shouted something to me, but I had gone into shock. I was spinning around in never-never land, not able to hear him, and feeling totally spaced out. Somehow, in those few minutes, my kneecap must have snapped back into place, and I snapped back into reality. I eventually got up, limped to the couch, and stayed there trying to figure out how I would accomplish the million things on my "to do" list that day. I was leaving for the concerts in Arizona in two days and there was still much to get done.

"You aren't thinking of actually going on this trip, are you?" was the million-dollar question from my dear friends. I, however, wouldn't even consider anything else. "Me? Cancel? Karen Drucker does not cancel gigs!" I was determined boldly and stubbornly to snap back. As the day went on and I was limping around, it started to hit me that this was a bigger undertaking than I had realized. The idea of schlepping through airports with my luggage and heavy CD bag, standing in those long security lines, and doing this all alone made me question my sanity. Yet the words "Karen Drucker DOES NOT CANCEL" kept ringing in my ears. However, as the day went on and my kneecap became more swollen, I had to consider the option of not going.

Suddenly, through the chatter in my brain and the sheer noise of all my "should's," a small faint light appeared with a vision of me sitting on my deck watching the clouds go by for an entire weekend. No responsibilities, no planes to catch, nothing to do. It's what my friend Maye calls "long thought time," where your mind can just wander without the threat of an interruption. I fantasized and watched the vision unfold, then got snapped back into reality thinking about how it would feel to call and cancel.

I made one exploratory phone call to Arizona to the person who had hired me. Upon hearing her nervous voice questioning me, I promptly went into my "knee jerk" reaction of appeasing her by saying, "Oh no, don't worry, I'll be fine. I just wanted to let you know I will be limping, can't stand up, and will be in pain. But don't you worry. Everything is just fine!"

The next day, I could barely get out of bed. I had to hop around to make my coffee, then hopped to the shower and hopped into my office. My husband took one look at little Miss Easter Bunny and read me the riot act for my stubbornness in this whole situation. I went to the doctor, and she also gave me the "Are you crazy?" lecture. I now had permission even from the doctor to cancel. Still, I stewed, I stressed, and then I finally did wake up. I realized that life will go on, these concerts will go on, that the world will go on if I say "No."

So I made the call, but I couldn't get the person who hired me on the phone. I knew that time was of the essence and that I couldn't wait for her to call me back, give me permission, tell me that it's okay and that I am not bad or unprofessional. I just had to do it. So I did. I cancelled. In that moment, the sky did not turn black; the winds did not begin to howl; life on earth as we know it did not change. I took care of myself. I gave myself a break, I lightened up, and I felt like a weight had been lifted off my shoulders. My knee "accident" had been this wonderfully executed opportunity for me to stop. To rest. To think, to feel, to just "be."

The next day I am sitting on my patio, watching the clouds go by and just having "long thoughts." Out of nowhere I hear a voice in my head that says, "It's time to move on."

"Move on?" I question. "What are you talking about?" I sit, I listen, and all of a sudden I feel this tightness in my stomach. Oh, that. Oh, the thing that I have been thinking about for a couple of years that I haven't really wanted to look at. That thing about leaving my secure, validating, wonderful church job as music director and going for my dream of being out in the world doing my music to a wider audience. Like a low hum you can hear but that doesn't affect your day-to-day life, this thought had been popping up from time to time. Whenever it did, I would get busy and squish it back down. My friend David, who has been a successful traveling musician for over twenty years, had been encouraging me to go for my dream. He made the point that what I wanted to do would be easy, fun, and profitable, that it was, simply, time for me to do it.

And yet how could I leave my secure job, the community who accepted me, and the special relationship I shared with the minister?

How could I do this? I couldn't, until the Universe allowed me the opportunity of having a spiritual two-by-four literally knock me down so I would stop long enough to listen. That weekend, I got quiet and prayed. I made lists, fretted, dreamed, and went through every emotion in the book. By Monday morning, I knew what I had to do. I called Reverend Karyl and made an appointment to meet with her that afternoon. I gave Karyl, the church, and myself time to transition and set the date to leave at the end of the year, six months away.

When the day came to finally move on, my emotions ran high. Reverend Karyl is a master of creating beautiful sacred rituals, and she had created a ritual of both releasing me to whatever my next step would be and welcoming in the new music director. She made a symbolic circle around the piano covering the floor with sheet music and invited me into the circle. I then sang a song to the congregation. Halfway through the song, I invited the new music director to come into the circle and continue playing the song as I prepared to leave. Karyl stood on the outside of the circle and first asked the congregation if they were willing to support me in leaving, knowing that this new experience was what I was being called to do. With their supportive "Yes!" she then held out her hand to me. "Are you ready to move on from this job and move out into the world to accept whatever is next for you to do?" she asked me.

With tears in my eyes, my heart pounding in my chest, and my whole body trembling, I reached out for her hand and walked out of the circle into my new life. I had no idea what was next, but I had said "Yes," and now I had to trust that my next step would be revealed.

"When you learn to say yes to yourself, you will be able to say no to others with love." — ALAN COHEN

N-O Is My New Yes

Words: Karen Drucker
Music: Karen Drucker & John Hoy

I've spent my life with the disease to please,
saying Yes when I really meant No.
Now I've seen the light and I feel the time is right,
there's something I need you to know...

> CHORUS:
> N-O is my new Yes. When I say No I'm saying Yes to me.
> N-O is my new Yes. When I say No I set myself free.

I've been living my life living to please,
full of effort and struggle and not enough ease.
I've been such a good girl, but now I know,
when I'm untrue to me I lose a piece of my soul.

> CHORUS

I thought to be liked I had to be nice,
doing what others wanted but I was paying the price.
'Cause what good is my giving, how authentic, how true,
when I cheat me just to please you?

> CHORUS

It's all about freedom. Having choices.
Trusting my heart to know, I can say Yes or I can say No.
I'll say Yes to what feels right, No to what feels wrong,
and when I'm undecided I'll just sing this little song. Come on!

> CHORUS

CHAPTER 16

We Are All Angels

Since I travel just about every weekend, I was thrilled when a conference that was on the East Coast was canceled and I had a weekend off. Hooray! No long five-hour flight, no schlepping all my CD's. I had a whole unplanned, free weekend! My euphoria lasted about a week, until I got a call from Sheryl. This bright, perky, enthusiastic voice brought out her Karen Drucker Fan Club pom-poms and gave me a song and dance about how it would be so wonderful if I came to Washington, D.C. to be the guest musician for her church's tenth anniversary celebration. "But Sheryl, it's my only weekend off in months and I am just fried," I whined.

"Oh, but pleasssssszzzzzzeeee!" Sheryl upped the ante. "We just looovvve your music, and it would make everybody sooooooo happy to have you here! You'd be giving everyone such a gift if you came to perform." Okay, I have a weak spot in the being-of-service department. So I agreed.

The day came, and off I went for my cross-country flight. I was picked up by Sheryl, who told me all about the weekend festivities. After dinner we drove over to see the church. I was a bit surprised when we drove up to an office building. I walked in and realized that their "church" was simply an office space with some chairs and a music stand for a pulpit.

"Oh my," I thought, visualizing the workshop, concert, and Sunday service I was there to provide. I have been so used to playing churches or conferences that had large buildings and were attended by tons of people that I had never thought to ask how big this church was. Obviously, it was small. However, I was there to do my job and give one-hundred percent, no matter how many people where there.

The next day I taught a music workshop and was introduced to the youngest member of the church, Kelsey. A painfully shy, gangly teenager, Kelsey wore a baseball cap down so low on her forehead that you actually never saw her eyes. She spoke in a whisper, eyes cast to the floor, toes pointed inward. I was told that she was thrilled to meet me and was a big fan, though her mother said she was being extra shy because she was a bit intimidated. I made a point all weekend long of talking to her, hugging her, having her help me sing a song in the workshop, and asking her opinion about what outfit I should wear for my concert. It wasn't anything much, just paying attention.

That night at my concert, as always, I sang a song called "We Are All Angels." During the song I pass out three halos to whoever catches my eye during the show. The halos are a simple headband with a fuzzy white ring that actually, from a distance, looks like a halo on your head, and I'm always amazed at people's reactions to the halos. Some people are so touched they get teary-eyed when I put the halo on their head; while others mumble something about how they are really the devil, or still others say they don't deserve it and I should give it to someone else. When I went up to Kelsey to give her the halo, I didn't know if I should put it on top of her baseball cap or just hand it to her. She hesitated for a moment, then took her baseball cap off, and I put the halo on her head. It was the first time I had really seen her. She had beautiful long hair and a sweet face. I went on with my show without giving much thought to what had just happened.

Later that evening, Kelsey's mother came to me with tears in her eyes saying how important that moment with the halo was. She told me that Kelsey never took off her hat. She had actually been wearing it for years, and no one at church had ever seen her without it. Her mom was even more amazed when Kelsey didn't put it back on for the rest of the evening. Even the next morning at church, there was no baseball cap.

As I was flying home, I realized that this had been my most favorite job of the entire year. I learned the important lesson from this loving community that a church has nothing to do with the number of people who attend, the size of the building, or anything other than the love and community felt by those who show up every Sunday. I also realized that my coming that long distance across the country really had nothing to do with teaching a workshop, giving a concert, or singing at their Sunday celebration. It was all about a young girl being reminded that she is beautiful just the way she is.

P.S. Her mom said that Kelsey never put the baseball cap on again after that weekend.

"We are each of us angels with only one wing, and we can only fly by embracing one another." — LUCIANO DE CRESCENZO

We Are All Angels

Words and Music: Karen Drucker and Michael Gott

CHORUS:
We are all angels who only have one wing.
We are all angels searching for each other.
All angels who cannot reach the sky,
'cause we need each other to fly.

Do you know that there are angels in our midst?
Can you hear them? Can you feel them?
They're all around you, with you everyday.
Do you see them or do you look the other way?
It's that man that I forgot to kiss as I hurried out the door,
or that stranger that said hello that I ignored.
They are angels. We are angels.

CHORUS

My life gets so busy, time goes by so fast.
I rush through the day trying to make each moment last.
But when I take the time to look around I see,
sweet angels are smiling back at me.
Everywhere at any time I need to open up my eyes,
and see the beauty that surrounds me and now I realize,
we are angels. We are angels.

CHORUS

We need each other to fly. We need each other to fly.

Part Two:
What Does Your Heart Have to Say?

CHAPTER 17

Calling All Angels

I remember getting the call from my sister, Tina. "Mom is in the hospital so we'd better go back there right away."

"Back there" referred to the radical move our mother made one year ago from Southern California to her childhood home of Poplar, Wisconsin. How she could trade 80-degree weather and palm trees for minus 20-degrees and snowdrifts was beyond me. But at this point in her life we supported her in anything she wanted to do. She was 78 years old and had terminal cancer and if she wanted to go back to her roots and live out her life in the country, well then, so be it. With my sister living in Southern California and me in Northern California, it was a challenge to hop on planes and visit her as frequently as we wanted. But we did it, until that fateful call when everything would change.

I was able to get a flight out on the same day and got to the hospital late that night. My mother looked so different than she had looked the last time I saw her. Her beautiful model's face, which was always so perfectly made-up, now appeared pale and tired. She had lost her thick gray hair and was bald from the chemo. But her eyes lit up as soon as I walked in the room. I was the "baby" and she took my face in her warm, smooth hands, stroked my face, and thanked me for coming. My sister would not be arriving until later that night, so my mother and I had some time together. We talked and laughed and cried. She hadn't spoken about death at all during any of her years of living with this disease. She had kept her usual positive attitude and did affirmations every morning, proclaiming her wellness. Her daily dose of saying "I Am Healed, Whole and Healthy" wound up becoming a chant that I wrote for her to listen to during her weekly chemo visits at the hospital.

But now it felt different. She knew something was changing, and in the pit of my stomach, so did I. She looked at me and for the first time admitted that she was afraid and asked me to help her with her fears. Holding her hand, looking deeply into her eyes, somehow I found the courage to say, "Mom, you brought me into this world. I will be here to help you out of it."

The next few days were a blur of more doctors coming and going, my sister and me trying to process what was happening, and eventually having the conversation with her oncologist about bringing in hospice care to help with this next stage.

My mother, like me, was a house nut. She loved fixing up her house, subscribing to house magazines, watching all those home and garden shows. So it was surprising when she decided that instead of going home to live out her last month or so, she wanted to go to a convalescent hospital. She had such wonderful memories of her house that she didn't want to see it look anything like a hospital, with nurses coming and going. So we found the best convalescent hospital in the area and moved her there the next day.

When she moved into the bare, generic room, she immediately gave my sister and me the assignment of bringing certain items she wanted from her house to liven up the drab room. With the precision of an architect, she made a chart to show which pictures went where on the walls, and within an hour the room had her touch and warmth. I was amazed to think back about the process involved in her having these few souvenirs and pictures she now wanted near her at the end of her life. Just one year ago, my sister and I had gone through the ordeal of moving her and seventy-seven years of "stuff" from Hollywood to Wisconsin. We hired a moving company with the largest van available, put into storage what wouldn't fit into the van, and tried to convince her that she didn't need to move every single thing in her house. Now, she was down to a few pictures of friends and family, and some mementos from her travels. And she was in a convalescent hospital.

Since my early twenties, I have entertained in many convalescent hospitals all around the Bay Area. Now all of a sudden, my
usually vivacious and active mother was one of those people and
I wanted to scream. It was all I could do to be cheerful and upbeat
when I went to see her there. I went every day. The very first day
I was there, I heard a soft but continuous beeping in the hallway
that would never stop. Having to listen to it was torture— pure
torture. Day and night, nurses would barge into the room without any concern for my mother's privacy. How could I keep up a
brave face for my mother when all I wanted was to just run away
and get her out of there?

With my mother now off chemo, she was gaining energy and
getting healthier than she had been in months. This was incred-
ibly confusing because, although the hospice nurses were telling
us that she only had about three to four weeks left to live, she
looked and sounded like her old self. We spent the days watching
food and home shows, talking, laughing, and doing painting projects. Life seemed "normal." I wanted to savor every moment with
her, so my sister and I would arrive as soon as our mother woke
up and stay until it was time to put her to bed. Luckily, Tina and
I were able to process our feelings during the one-hour drive back
to her house that we had each night.

Each afternoon when my mother took a nap, my sister and I
would have a little "personal time." I would spend every moment
"off" in the recreation room at the end of the hall where there
was a beat-up old piano stuck in the corner. I found that just playing and singing for a few minutes every day would calm me down
and I wound up writing a bunch of songs and chants during those
times. One day I was playing and softly singing to myself when I
felt a presence around me. I turned to find twenty or so people
in wheelchairs. They had wheeled themselves in to listen to my
"concert." After that I realized my " private time" at the piano
was no longer—and I would daily give little concerts to whoever
wanted to hear a song.

As the weeks passed, my mother did eventually change, and
as predicted by the hospice nurses she went through the steps

associated with letting go of life. She had less energy, would sleep much more, wouldn't want to talk as much, and generally started to go deeper inside herself. There would be times at night where she would awake with a start and say there was someone in the room with her. She was convinced it was her mother, or maybe my father talking to her. To ease her mind, I would just tell her that these were her angels who were letting her know she was safe and that they would greet her when she passed over. She would find comfort in that and gently go back to sleep.

My mother was a wonderful and talented painter and photographer. In those last weeks she had been painting little plaster figurines. She had painted some angels but it was the little Santa Claus with his big red belly and knapsack that she was working on this final week. Those last few days when she could barely get out of bed, I was so moved to see the determination in her to finish this Santa Claus and put the final touches on him. Without saying a word and living in her own world now, she would paint his belt and his beard with great precision and then get tired and have to go back to bed.

On the final day of her life, her last act was getting out of bed one more time, to put the finishing touches on Santa's perfect little brown shoes. After that she was done. I remember her looking at it, smiling, and then asking to be brought back to bed, where she smiled at us and closed her eyes. My mother died in the wee hours of that night with my sister and me by her side.

She was an artist and inspiration to me until the end.

Marjorie Ann Drucker
October 25, 1923 - September 27, 2003

"While we are sleeping, angels have conversations with our souls."

AUTHOR UNKNOWN

For my mom

Calling All Angels

Words & Music: Karen Drucker

I'm calling all angels to surround the one I love.
Let her know she is safe and taken care of.
Hold her hand and rock her and whisper in her ear,
that angels now surround her, there's nothing to fear.

I'm calling all angels can you help me to let go,
and understand the meaning of the words "I don't know."
I've been walking right beside her but her path will be alone.
So I'm calling all angels to lead her home.

Let her know that she is safe.
Let her know that she is loved.
Let her hold on to your wings of faith and help her to fly.

I'm calling all angels surround her in your light.
I can feel that you are with her,
even though you're out of sight.
Let her feel your warm embrace as you lead her on her way.
I'm calling all angels to be with her today.
I'm calling all angels...Calling all angels...

CHAPTER 18

Listen to the Children: What Does Your Heart Have to Say?

I remember walking into the hospital and taking a deep breath. Those familiar sensations I felt when visiting my mother in the convalescent hospital were happening to me all over again: my stomach was tightening, I was feeling kind of nauseous, and basically I wanted to turn right around and get out of there. I was about to do a show at Oakland Children's Hospital and even though I had been singing in hospitals and convalescent homes for Bread & Roses since my early twenties, I knew it would take every amount of performing experience to make it through.

Bread & Roses, an organization that offers free live entertainment for people confined in institutions, such as hospitals, prisons, and recovery centers, was started in the San Francisco Bay Area in 1974 by singer/songwriter Mimi Fariña. A successful recording artist, Mimi had suddenly been dropped by her record label. She searched her soul to find how her music could still have a place in the world. With the initial help of some of her famous friends, along with her sister, Joan Baez, Mimi formed Bread & Roses with the intention to take performers into institutions where people do not have the ability to go out to hear live music. Bread & Roses produced a big benefit concert once a year to help fund the organization and took performers like me into these institutions to entertain. Today Bread & Roses uses a tagline which says "Hope and Healing through Live Music." That's what the organization does now, and that's what it did from the beginning. Little did I know when I first started with them how it would influence the direction my musical path would take.

Being young, enthusiastic, and very inexperienced, I said yes to every gig they called me to do. Whether convalescent homes, recovery centers, AIDS wards, or lockdown psychiatric units—you name it—I would be there trying to make some kind of difference to these people with my little shows.

As the years went on, I became known in the organization as one of the "troopers," someone to whom they could give the harder shows. One time I sang at a psych ward where they locked the big metal doors behind me and where all of the windows were covered with bars. Some of the people in my audience were in strait jackets. I was just left in the room with a little piano, seriously wondering what I was doing. I remember making the worst mistake that day, which was starting off my show with the Crosby, Stills, Nash and Young song, "Love the One You're With." As I sang the opening line, "If you're down and confused, and you don't remember who you're talking to," I quickly realized that most of my audience were actually talking to themselves and I'd better pick another song—fast!

My specialty for Bread & Roses was singing in convalescent homes, and it was great experience. Even if I was not so great or was singing off key, the people were not going to throw things at me or go anywhere. The attendants would wheel about twenty patients into the recreation room and clamp the locks down on their wheelchairs so they couldn't wheel themselves away. At some facilities, this would signal a much-needed break for the staff, and they would just leave me there to babysit the patients during my thirty-minute show. Other facilities would have a staff who were very engaged with the patients and truly cared, and the level of responsiveness was quite different.

I would sing all the old standards from the 30's and 40's. People loved hearing their favorite songs, and would pinch my cheeks and tell me how cute I was and how I looked just like their grandkids. I was warm and sweet with these people and simply got used to the horrible smells, the depressing lighting, and some of my audience yelling at the top of their lungs, "I want out!!!" I even had one moment when I bent down to hold the hand of a sweet older woman while singing, "The Nearness of You," only to find that the warm sensation I felt on my feet was none other than her urinating on me. In other words, I received lots of performing experience in these kinds of places.

When I first started singing at convalescent homes, I would direct my attention to the people who appeared interested and "with it." If they responded to me, then I would respond to them. But over the years of doing these shows I noticed that if I could just move past my fears and make some kind of connection with the ones who did not seem "with it," that would make all the difference for me and my heart would open. I would try to see behind the outward physical appearance of those who were hard to look at because of their physical deformities, and I gave equal attention to the people in the back of the room who were in their own world. There was one woman with a huge swollen tongue. Her head drooped onto her chest and she was drooling. I didn't know if she would respond. But when I bent down in front of her and gingerly took her hand while singing "Over the Rainbow," it was as if a light switch had come on. Her eyes lit up and she started humming along with me. Moments like those made it all worth it, and I learned that music truly is a bridge that can connect hearts.

As I walked into the pediatric ward at Oakland's Children's Hospital, I needed to remember all that I had learned. This was different from all those other shows. This time I would be singing to children, many of them hooked up to medical devices. Some were bald from their chemo treatments, and some were clearly struggling to survive. I was there to perform with my friend Robin Goodrow, an Emmy award-winning actress/writer who had a successful children's television show called "Buster and Me." Robin had signed up to be a Bread & Roses performer around the same time as me, and we decided to combine our talents and perform at these children's hospitals together.

After setting up a makeshift puppet stage, Robin would go behind it with her very large monkey-puppet, Vanilla. Our act was performing skits and songs, and just allowing the children the opportunity to talk to Vanilla. My character in our little play was called Dr. Heart. I was dressed from head to toe in red and white, with a big smock that displayed a giant heart, heart sox, and multicolored pants and shoes. The main line I would say, over and over, while putting my stethoscope to a child's heart, would be, "What does your heart have to say?"

Looking out at this audience of sweet innocent faces was an emotional challenge whenever we played these hospitals. And yet, to see them light up, and possibly to feel like a normal kid when we performed, was the reward every time. When I would ask them, "What does your heart have to say," many of them felt the freedom to say to Vanilla what they couldn't say to their parents or nurses. It would take all my acting training to stay in character and not start to cry as they would tell Vanilla about their fears of dying, or how they didn't want their parents to worry about them, or how they just wanted to go out and play. I learned so much from these wise children. These were probably the most heart-opening and rewarding times of performing that I have ever had.

I have used Dr. Heart's question over and over in my life. When I am scared, stuck, confused, or at a crossroad in my life, I imagine putting that toy stethoscope to my heart and simply asking, "What does your heart have to say?"

For more information about Bread & Roses visit their website: www.breadandroses.org.

"Children are the bridge to heaven." — PERSIAN PROVERB

Listen to the Children

Words: Karen Drucker & Roberta Rigney
Music: Karen Drucker

CHORUS:
Listen to the children.
Listen to the children.
Listen to the children, 'cause they're the ones who know.

Listen to the children 'cause they're the ones who see,
all of the life, beauty and love, the children hold the key.
They can teach us how to view the world through eyes of peace.
When we listen to the children then we'll see.

CHORUS

Listen to the children 'cause they're the ones who hear,
all of the joy, music and laughter, the children have no fear.
They can teach us how to let the love of God be near.
When we listen to the childen then we'll hear.

CHORUS

CHAPTER 19

The Christmas Present

It was Christmas Eve, and I was crabby. Justifiably crabby. I had agreed to sing one last time at the church that I was no longer music director of, performing for their Christmas Eve service. I had worked every Christmas Eve for the past ten years as a church music director, but this year felt different.

My mother had passed away two months earlier. I remembered how last year I had made the decision not to fly back to Wisconsin to be with her on Christmas since this would be my last "duty" as the music director at the church. I would be leaving my position at the end of the year, so I felt obligated to be there. That was the key word: obligated. So here I was, again, "obligated" to work on this night when everyone else is having dinner with friends and family and celebrating this holiday. Okay, maybe some of this had to do with Mom being gone. The guilt I felt about not being with her last year was huge, since it would have been my last Christmas with her. How was I to know that? But still I felt anger at myself for not saying no to working, sadness at her not being here anymore, and lots of other emotions, all covered up by the veil of just being crabby.

My wonderful husband, who is my favorite musician to work with, agreed to come and perform the service with me and it totally changed the experience. Rehearsing that afternoon, we found a few sweet Christmas songs that brought us both to tears. I began to see that I needed to reframe this whole evening and put it in a new light.

That night as we performed and I looked out over the crowd who were holding little candles and sweetly singing "Silent Night," my heart started to thaw and a lump came into my throat. Thankfully everyone knew the words enough so when I couldn't sing they just kept on singing without me.

In that moment I reflected on the emotional roller coaster of this day, and I wondered how often I have one emotion (my crabbiness) which is actually a cover-up for what's really going on (my sadness). I wondered about how I could access that real emotion earlier instead of having hours, days or years of not really knowing what I am feeling. It was a great lesson on that Christmas Eve.

The service was over, and we had a great time. I thought that was it, until we decided to go to dinner. The place that I was sure would be open, my favorite Jewish deli, was closed (a Jewish deli closed on Christmas Eve? Go figure!) but we saw people coming out of a restaurant across the street, so we took our chances.

We got in with five minutes to spare before an early closing time. We were seated and were thrilled with our good luck. Just then we both overheard a waitress complain to another waitress about a large group of people stiffing her on what should have been a sizeable tip. I don't know how I sensed it but I just had this vivid impression that she was a single mom with kids who was probably feeling the money crunch of Christmas. In the same moment, John and I were both moved to do something radical. We each took out ten dollars and I went up to her and said, "It's Christmas Eve and we just heard what you said. We would like to make up the tip those people should have left for you and we hope you'll accept this gift." Her mouth fell open and tears came to her eyes.

We both felt the connection. That's when I got the real Christmas present, the true meaning of Christmas Spirit. Maybe this is what it is really all about. It's not about running out to a ton of stores, buying stuff for my friends who already complain about having too much stuff, and getting caught up in all of the stress that accompanies this season. Christmas Spirit is simply about connection—connection with my family, my friends, and even strangers that come into my life, maybe a waitress who needs a little validation. John and I didn't do that gesture to "get" anything, but in that moment we both trusted our hearts and, in so doing, we were all transformed.

The unexpected perk that followed was that she turned out to be our waitress and treated us like the King and Queen of England. She didn't need to do that, because our payment was the look in her eyes every time she talked to us and shared about the presents she had bought for her kids. We wound up having a lovely dinner and left the restaurant feeling inspired and filled with Christmas Spirit.

Maybe this was going to be a nice Christmas after all.

"Christmas is not a time nor a season, but a state of mind. To cherish peace and goodwill, to be plenteous in mercy, is to have the real spirit of Christmas." — CALVIN COOLIDGE

Christmas Lullaby

Words: Karen Drucker
Music: John R. Burr

Late in the evening when everything's quiet,
I can hold you close in my dreams.
I can feel you around me and hear your sweet laughter,
and I know that I'm not alone,
You are my deep soul connection,
and you are always here in my heart.
When I think of you, you heal my soul.
You rock me and soothe me like a Christmas lullaby.

CHAPTER 20

My Religion Is Kindness

I have finally realized that the process of being kind, or doing nice things for people, can be totally selfish. Yep—selfish. I realize that doing an unexpected kindness for someone might make that person feel good, but the truth is it makes me feel great. Let me give you some examples. The first one, just as in "The Christmas Present," also involves a tip that was very appreciated, but which meant much more to the giver than the recipient.

It's 7:00 a.m. and I am schlepping my bags through the throngs of people at San Francisco International Airport. I am traveling to a gig where the end result of my day will be twelve hours of flying, waiting, and more schlepping. I am not in a particularly good mood, mainly because I had to wake up at 4:30 this morning to be here by 7:00 a.m. I am not really a happy traveler. I check in, get my boarding pass, and head off to get breakfast, hoping that a good cup of coffee will brighten my mood. I am sitting next to four guys with foreign accents who are having cheeseburgers and beer at 7:00 a.m. Yuck!

The waitress, an older Chinese woman, is very sweet and brings me my coffee and breakfast. At the end of my meal I overhear her explaining to the cheeseburger guys that a one-dollar tip is not the way we do it in the U.S. She shows them on my bill that I had left her a twenty percent tip, and suggests this to them as an example. After she leaves them, I see them roll their eyes and then rush out the door laughing. Coming back to their table, she sees she's been stiffed. I realize in that moment that I can just walk away, or I can do something. At first, I think, hey, I gave a generous tip. What more can I do? But then I feel a call to help in some way. I pull out a few more dollars and give it to her, saying, "I'm sorry those people were rude to you. Maybe this will make up for it." She looks at me with tears in her eyes and says I have made her day.

Was I trying to save the world? No. The bottom line is that I had experienced a total attitude change. I came into that restaurant feeling crabby, and now I felt better. The Dalai Lama says, "When we feel love and kindness toward others, it not only makes others feel loved and cared for, but it helps us also to develop inner happiness and peace." Did this act of kindness change the specific events of my day? Well, no, I still had a long day in front of me. However, now those hours didn't seem quite so bad after all.

Since that day, I have taken this idea a step further. I now carry ten one-dollar bills whenever I travel with the intention to do random acts of kindness throughout the weekend. The goal is for the ten dollars to be gone before I return home.

I can use the money for anything I want. This last weekend in Seattle, a woman asked if I could use my room key to unlock the door to the vending machines. Not only couldn't she find her room key, but she was fumbling around trying to find her money so she could buy a soda. After I opened the door for her, I handed her a dollar bill and said, "Here. The Coke is on me." Now this was just a dollar, but her shocked look and sweet expression was worth a hundred dollars to me.

I have found that my little ritual works well in Starbucks. Recently, a woman who was in front of me in line ordered her coffee and when I told her I would like to treat her, she looked at me like I had three heads. "Why would you want to do a thing like that?" she protested. "Give the money to someone who really needs it, I'm fine!" We went back and forth for a minute until I said in my best New York accent: "It's just a cuppa cooffeee — it's no big deal!" She finally relented, and I bought her coffee. As we stood there together waiting for our orders, she turned to me and said with the softest and sweetest expression on her face, "You know, no one does things like this for me. Thank you so much."

I felt like that simple act had made a difference for her— and especially for me.

These are all little acts, but being aware and conscious of being kind has become a spiritual practice for me. So next time we're in line together at Starbucks, I might just buy your coffee!

"Kindness does wonderful things to a face." — DIXIE DOYLE

My Religion Is Kindness

Words & Music: Karen Drucker

INSPIRED BY JOAN BORYSENKO

CHORUS:
My religion is kindness. My church is nature.
My God is a feeling that lives deep inside.
My job is to be conscious. My path is forgiveness.
My religion is kindness and I practice it every day.

Everyone has a story. Everyone has pain.
When we strip away our masks we find
that we're really all the same.
It's those little things we say and do that can mean so much.
It's a smile, a connection, a simple loving touch.

CHORUS

Today I'm gonna ask myself what more can I do,
to be a radiant child of God and let my love shine through.
I'm gonna let my heart be my guide to give the best of me.
I'm gonna share joy, share my love, give it boundlessly.

CHORUS

Jack and Jill went up the hill to fetch a pail of water.
But then Jack fell down and broke his crown
and Jill came running after.
She said "Jack tell me what can I do to help ease your mind?"
He said "Hold my hand and just be kind and I know I'll be fine."

CHORUS

CHAPTER 21

You Are My Family

As a kid I always loved riding my bike. It wasn't so much because of how good the exercise would feel or that it would be a welcome change from the long, boring swim workouts I did daily. It was more that my bike represented freedom. As a teenager, I felt like I was held captive on top of the mountain in the Hollywood Hills with no other kids to play with and no malls to hang out in. When I saved up all my money and got my shiny blue Schwinn ten-speed, the world opened up for me. I could ride down the hill and be a normal teenager.

As an adult, I continued riding for fun. However, it wasn't until I saw a sign in a coffee shop window that I realized why I had been riding my bike all those years. The sign was about an event that was being organized in the Bay Area. It said you could do a seven-day, 560-mile bike ride for AIDS, riding from San Francisco to Los Angeles, and make a difference. The "make a difference" got me. I had already lost several close friends to this disease, and I felt helpless in the face of such a huge problem. I was excited that I could actually make a difference by riding my bike and raising money for AIDS research. The date was six months away, and I immediately knew that that ride had my name on it.

Having trained all of my life for various athletic events, I knew exactly what the training would entail and went at it like it was a job. I was on my bike at least five days a week, increasing my time and miles daily. Eventually, I hooked up with other riders for organized rides that would have us biking all over the Bay Area in all kinds of weather. These training rides got more intense as we got closer to the date, and I amazed myself when I realized I had worked myself up to being able to ride 80 to 100 miles in a day.

It wasn't easy, though. I remember one ride in which about twenty-five of us started out together around 8:00 a.m. Because I was slow and steady, I would see everyone pass me by and leave me in the dust. There was one large mountain around mile 75 that was really steep, and it seemed like the switchbacks would never end. It was the ultimate test of my mental ability. I would stop and cry, swearing that I would never do this again. I'd look longingly at cars that passed by, hoping the drivers would take pity and just pick me up. None of them did, and I had no choice but to keep going. I eventually coasted to my car at around 7:00 p.m., when all the other riders were long gone. I peeled myself off my bike, broke down sobbing, and seriously asked myself whether or not I was nuts to be doing this. Then I treated myself to a big, greasy cheeseburger, fries, and ice cream. There had to be some kind of reward for this day of torture!

When the day came to start the AIDS ride, I was riding high on pure adrenaline. Hundreds of people were at the starting point at Fort Mason in San Francisco. Riders, supporters, and news people showed up, as well as my favorites, The Sisters of Perpetual Indulgence. The "Sisters" were a group of men dressed up like nuns who ran around sprinkling fairy dust on all of us, blessing our rides. There were other men in full drag, kids, grandmothers, and AIDS groups with signs saying, "Thank you for doing this for us." It was the first of many times I would really understand the fact that this was about a whole lot more than just me riding my little bike.

When I looked around at my fellow riders, I saw everything you could imagine. Professional riders decked out in their corporate sponsored bike attire, guys in drag with feather boas and glittery high heels, teenagers who looked like they had just woken up and hopped on an old bike they grabbed out of the garage. There were single people, married people, straight, gay, black, white, Asian, Latino, Republicans, Democrats. We were all there, putting any differences aside, ready as a group to do this ride for a greater purpose.

When more than 2,600 of us took off, it was the most exhilarating feeling I had ever felt as an athlete. People lined the streets of San Francisco cheering, applauding, holding signs, and blowing kisses. The first twenty miles that day went by in an instant. It wasn't until my first big hill, when all the crowds were gone, that I was left alone with my own huffing and puffing and the thoughts of what lay in front of me for the next seven days, and what I had gotten myself into.

One of the main rules of the ride was that you had to ride single file, so you would pass people by shouting out, "On your left." This rule really forced you not to talk to anyone, and there were hours and hours when I would be alone with my thoughts. One fellow rider said it was the most intense therapy he had done in years, just being with himself for so many days.

We would travel on some major highways, but most of the time we took the backroads through the central valley of California, through pastures, and through small forgotten towns. I had a lot of time to think about what this whole event meant and about all the people who were doing it with me. Often someone would be riding in front of me with a T-shirt that said "I am riding in the memory of...," and there would be a picture of their wife, or sister, or brother who had died from AIDS. As we silently rode along, my thoughts would go to that person riding in support of someone they loved who had died, and I wondered what they were feeling at that moment.

When I got pledges for the ride, I made up my own T-shirt. On the back it said "Backing me all the way to L.A.," along with the names of the people who were providing financial support. On the front I drew a big heart with the heading "In Memory Of," and wrote the names my supporters had given me of their loved ones who had lost their lives to AIDS. In the center of the heart was the name of a high school friend I had lost—David Montalbano. When I was sixteen and feeling so insecure and like an outcast, David was the friend who took me to the prom, encouraged me to audition for the high school play, and made me laugh constantly. When he died from AIDS in his early twenties, I was devastated. I felt that I carried David and all of these names in my heart and that I rode in their honor. Having those names on my shirt gave me a feeling of empowerment and purpose, and kept me going in the long days ahead.

Riding with so many people for such a long distance was a challenge for me. Since I was such a slow but steady rider, I discovered that to be in by the cutoff time of dusk every night, I would have to be on the road early. I would wake up at 5:30 a.m. to be on my bike by 7:00. I would ride for a few hours before the first "rest stop." To say these stops were colorful and entertaining ways to rest would be a mild understatement. Each "crew" would have a theme to their pit stop, and each of the stops would try to outdo one another. At one pit stop I was greeted by men in drag with names like Miss Guided, Miss DeMeanor, and Miss Treats. Another time I was cold, hungry and tired when I saw, in the distance through the blowing fog, a man in a hula skirt with coconuts over his chest, swaying a huge palm leaf in the wind and beckoning me to come to his Shangri-La. The whole pit stop, which was in the middle of a cow pasture, was set up to look like Gilligan's Island and the pit crew were all dressed as characters from the show. I know there must have been huge fights as to who would be Ginger, and sure enough, there was a man in full drag with a feather boa, sequined dress, and high heels, handing me a Cliff Bar and Gatorade, and instructing me in that breathy Ginger-like voice where to go next.

I would take a few minutes to stand in line for the Porta-Potties, get a snack, and then load up on "butt balm," which was a weird mixture of some kind of lanolin that you would discreetly stick on your nether regions to help with the chafing that comes from being on a bike for eight hours a day. After comparing experiences with a few people, encouraging others and whining a bit, I would get on my bike and ride until the next unique pit stop.

After I had ridden anywhere from fifty to ninety miles in a day, I would be so tired that I would try to coast as much as possible towards the daily finish line. However, once I reached the finish line, the real work would begin. I would lock up my bike, stand in line to get the two-person tent, walk forever to find the marker for where to set it up, break down in tears from frustration over how to put it together, and walk for what seemed like forever to the semi-trucks to find my personal gear. By now I was cursing myself for packing so much personal stuff because I had to haul it all the way back to my tent after the strenuous day of riding. Once I got my gear back to my tent I would then get in line for the toilet, get in line for the shower, get in line for the food, and then walk back in the dark trying to find my own, identical-looking tent that I had set up three hours ago. When I finally found my tent, my "roommate" would be snoring like a freight train, while the person in the tent next to me had a jumpy foot that kept kicking me as I tried to sleep. I did this for seven days. What fun!

Every once in a while it would all be too much. The daily wear and tear on my body, lack of sleep, and simply being with so many people would make me crack. But just when I thought I couldn't take it anymore, I would find my inspiration in Dave. Dave was this great guy who had lost both of his legs and was riding a custom-built bike that he "pedaled" with his arms. Anytime I would feel some internal whining about to surface, Dave would pedal by me with a big smile. I would immediately say to myself, "Get over it, Drucker!" and hop right back on my bike with a new attitude.

Other inspirations were the Positive Peddlers, a group of people living with the disease and doing the ride to educate people about AIDS, and the "Chicken Lady," a man so dedicated to the fight that he made a commitment to do all of the AIDS rides around the country (about five rides a year). The fact that he would dress up like a chicken with a beak and feathers on his head just made it more fun. All of these people would motivate me, but it was the strangers and supporters who melted my heart. We would be riding along and all of a sudden, written in chalk on the road, would be staggered messages like, "You...are ...helping ...me ...to ...stay alive ...Thank....You!!!! There were small towns that gave all of us red ribbons and welcomed us like heroes, and farm workers we passed who would donate money to the cause. I got used to crying and riding.

This ride was very profound for me. We were 2,613 people with a crew of 674, riding down the length of California as one. I felt that even though I was only one person, my small part of this huge group made a big difference. There would be times when a huge hill would take everything out of me, but all of a sudden another rider would come alongside saying, "Come on you can do it—you're almost there." It got to be customary to get to the top of a hill, take a gulp of water, and then ride back down to encourage the other riders coming up, just as someone had done for me.

We needed each other to make this trip and to make a difference, and we did. Each of us was asked to raise $2,500 in pledges to participate in the event. I personally raised $5,000, and we as a group raised the most money that had ever been raised by a single sporting event at that time: $9.5 million.

By the time we rode into the closing ceremony, as one, wearing the rainbow shirts we were all given, each and every one of us was changed forever. We had voted that Dave, the man with no legs, would be the first to ride into the ceremony. So with Dave out in front, and with the "Rocky" theme music blaring over the loud speakers, 2,613 of us rode our bikes into Century City in Los Angeles to the cheers and tears of hundreds of supporters. Tears were streaming down my face, and my heart was filled with love and gratitude for these strangers who were now part of my family.

I started out just being rider number 2,366, but I finished feeling like I had a new family and that I had made a difference.

"Call it a clan, call it a network, call it a tribe, call it a family. Whatever you call it, whoever you are, you need one." — JANE HOWARD

You Are My Family

Words: Karen Drucker
Music: Karen Drucker & John Hoy

I don't care if you're straight.
I don't care if you're gay.
I don't care who you love.
I'm here to love you anyway.
I don't care if you're black.
I don't care if you're white.
I don't care what color you are.
I'm here to love you with all my might.

> CHORUS:
> You are my sister.
> You are my brother.
> You are a part of me.
> Let's face it, you are my family.

I don't care if you're thin.
I don't care if you're fat.
I don't care what you eat.
My love is so much larger than that.
I don't care if you're rich.
I don't care if you're poor.
I don't care how much money you got.
Loving you is what I was put here for.

> CHORUS

There's no difference between you and me.
No boundaries as far as I can see.
No separation or alienation. We are all one.

> CHORUS

CHAPTER 22

You Are Loved

I ordered my Grande Soy Latte and low-fat oat fruit scone from Starbucks. Today I was doing something different— not running off, but actually sitting and reading a book and savoring my coffee. I even asked for it in a mug instead of the paper to-go cup. Radical behavior for me.

I sat down and read my book, looking up every once in a while to notice the yuppies, the teenagers (when did thirteen-year-olds start drinking coffee?!), the mom circles who met every morning with their kids in strollers, and the other people like me, who normally dash in and out in three minutes to get their morning fix.

But today was different. I wanted to just "be," to take time, to not rush. My ears perked up to hear "Home," an old favorite Bonnie Raitt song over the house speakers: "And home sings me of sweet things, my life there has its own wings. Fly over the mountains, though I'm standing still." In an instant I was transported back in time. I was twenty-two years old, sitting on the middle metal hump of my friend Brian's beat up van. It was Brian, my boyfriend Craig, and I, driving up to participate at a music camp near Lake Tahoe. I was young, excited to learn everything about music, and just imagining in my wildest dreams that I could ever make a living as a musician. The music was blasting, the warm wind was blowing through the van, and life was simple and good.

Suddenly I was back in Starbucks with tears streaming down my face. Brian, my friend for more than thirty years, had passed away in his sleep of a heart attack just a few days before, and that song had opened up my heart to a flood of memories that I didn't even know I had.

I had gotten "the call" on a March morning. I had been making my coffee, and the phone rang at the ungodly hour of 7:00 a.m. I checked the name on the caller ID and seeing it was Brian, I picked up the phone with an enthusiastic, "Baby cakes—I miss you! Why the heck are you calling me so early?" There was silence on the other end, until I heard his wife, Kim, whisper my name. In that moment I knew something had happened to Brian, and I went into a tailspin.

It was now a week later, and as I sat in Starbucks and hid my face in my book, I just let myself feel all the emotions. I have long since learned that the expression, "Whatever you resist persists," is so true. I knew that if I didn't ride the waves of grief when they were here, it would lead to my having some kind of meltdown six months from now in a random moment, like while waiting in a line at Macy's. I remembered Brian's laugh, his humor, and his Irish anger, which would burst out if someone had pushed him too far. But it was truly his laugh that I could literally feel in my soul.

The next week was Brian's funeral. I don't think he would have really wanted a big Catholic mass, but Brian's parents, distraught beyond belief, held a grand formal event at their church. Everyone turned out, including people I had not seen in twenty years, and all the musicians with whom Brian had worked over the years. We were all there as a musical community that came together to cry, laugh, share stories, and lean on one another in disbelief that one of our own was gone. I think I would have handled it better if he had been older. I guess I held an unconscious belief about it being kind of okay to die when someone was in their 80's or 90's and had lived a long full life, but fifty was my age and too young and too scary. This was just too out of left field. I had Brian on my list to call that week about going out to lunch and catching up, and now he was gone. So much for plans.

As I sat in the enormous church, the thing that I was most taken with was how Brian would have reacted to all of this. He would have been blown away and, quite frankly, I think he would have been stunned. Three hundred people were there to say what a difference he had made in their lives, how unique he was, and the kindnesses he had shown them. Yet I think he never really understood how special he was. Everyone talked about his accomplishments, but I knew about his frustrations at not really doing what he wanted to do. There was a part of him that just didn't believe he was good enough or worthy enough to really go for his dreams. He actually was just starting to do that, but life had other plans.

I wondered how many of us really know how much we are loved? How often does that voice of "not enough" or "try harder" or "If I could just (fill in the blank), then I'll be okay," come up and keep us from really feeling loved? What would it look like, feel like, if we could just dump the whole try-harder game and just accept our own talents, beauty, worthiness? It's something I am still working on within myself, and I saw it from a whole new perspective that day at Brian's funeral.

This period of time, since getting the call that March morning, has been like entering a new land. There is vulnerability, an uneasiness about life, for me. The secure belief that I had it "all under control" is gone. Poof. I realize I never had it under control in the first place, that nothing in life is guaranteed. But that phone call just burst the bubble in me that was all about illusion and thinking I had it all scoped out.

The other night I was part of a concert that, to my surprise, was outside in the dirt. I had to walk from my seat to the stage, and since I hadn't gotten the memo from the event organizers, was wearing all white with high heels. I navigated slowly, aware of every rock and pebble so as to not wind up face down in the dirt or twist my ankle. I realize that this is what I am doing now in my life, navigating slowly. I am more aware of every person and every event, realizing the preciousness in everything and going more slowly to take it all in.

I believe that there are gifts in death and I believe that Brian's gift to all of us is to open up to how loved we really are; to take the time to let the people in our lives know how much we love them and not to wait, because you never know if you will get that chance again.

Brian made a big difference in his time of being here, whether he knew it or not. Now it's up to me to do the same.

"You yourself, as much as anybody in the entire universe, deserve your love and affection." — BUDDHA

You Are Loved

Words: Karen Drucker
Music: Karen Drucker & John Hoy

Here it comes again, that feeling of not enough.
I see you struggle, I feel your pain.
How can I convince you that you are a radiant child of God?
You are worthy, deserving, loving and caring, a shining light of love.

> CHORUS:
> If only you could see yourself as other people do.
> You would see the light of love that shines to everyone.
> You would understand the reason why people care for you.
> You would see that, you would know that you are loved.

You look in the mirror and all you do is criticize.
But take another look and see the soul that's in your eyes.
You have everything you need, it's all inside of you.
Step into your power, open your heart, and let your love shine through.

> CHORUS

CHAPTER 23

Breathe

I created a miracle this morning while checking in for my flight to Kansas City. I am on my way to a seven-day music conference where I will perform three concerts, do a TV show, teach two workshops, and be in front of many people every day. That's a lot of days, and a lot of different clothes. So it figures that, despite all of my clothes-planning, all the choosing and re-choosing of outfits, I could have easily exceeded the fifty-pound weight limit for baggage set by the airline.

I held my breath as the ticket agent weighed my bag. I could just imagine having to squat down in front of the long line of impatient people, trying to repack so my bag would be deemed the acceptable weight. I guess my good karma paid off in this moment because, if the bag was over the weight limit, the ticket agent let it slide. She didn't know that my other bag, containing all of the CD's I was bringing to sell at the conference, might even be heavier than the first bag. But lo and behold—it was exactly fifty pounds!

Every time I fly, I am always amazed and in awe of the people who know how to travel lightly. They come on the plane with a five-hour flight ahead of them, and bring nothing more than a paperback book or sometimes nothing at all. Some of them sit down, fold their hands in their laps, and simply close their eyes. Some look out the window and some go to sleep, while others just sit there and breathe. I want to turn to them and ask what kind of spiritual path they are on that they can be so content to just "be" for this entire flight.

I sometimes think to myself, here I am, practicing the art of "being here now," of living simply, of being this spiritual person, and yet I bring enough stuff on the plane to be occupied for a trip to China, though my flights are usually just a couple of hours! God forbid I don't have the current *People* magazine, my computer with all of the work I didn't get done this week, songs to write, past projects that I need to finish—and then there's the food. I have my nuts, my PowerBars, crackers, water. I mean, what would happen if I actually didn't eat for a few hours? You'd think I was going on some kind of marathon survival trip and had to bring all of my worldly belongings with me, but no—there is more at home!

The funniest thing about all of this it that one of my favorite books is *Clear Your Clutter*, by Karen Kingston, in which she speaks of the joy of living simply and getting rid of stuff. My favorite pastime at home is clutter clearing and weeding out what I no longer need. I just never thought it applied to me when I travel. So maybe next time you see me on the plane I might be one of those Zen travelers content to just sit and be, and breathe, and gaze out the window having long uninterrupted thoughts.

"Becoming aware of your own breath forces you into the present moment—the key to all inner transformation. Whenever you are conscious of the breath, you are absolutely present."

ECKHART TOLLE

Breathe

Words & Music: Karen Drucker

I breathe in. I breathe out.
I take in. I give out.
I let love. I let go.
I release. I know.

I forgive. I receive.
I can feel. I believe.
I am healed. I am whole.
I release. I know.

CHORUS: Breathe. Breathe...

No need to push. No need to try.
No need to worry or question why.
Surrender. Let go.
Release and know.

CHORUS: Breathe. Breathe...

CHAPTER 24

Gentle with Myself

When I was in my twenties I did the whole spiritual enlightenment thing, including signing up for the EST training. I took all the classes they offered-everything from making my relationships work, to dealing with money, to achieving all of my goals. I even signed up for the six-day intensive where the highlight of the week was rappelling down mountains. I did deep personal processes and challenged myself like I had never done before.

There was one particular exercise in that very intense six-day period which profoundly affected me and which I remind myself of to this day. It was simply the morning run. My group of about sixty people, all ages, body types and excuses, had to run one mile every morning. That was it. The people in charge would start us off and someone at the end would call out our times as we ran across the finish line No judgment, no discussion. Just run, and then receive our time for the day. Just run—whatever that meant to you. Some people whined; some people just did it; some people walked; some people sprinted like it was their Olympic moment. I did it like I do everything, meaning I made a big deal about it in my mind and challenged myself to better my time each day. Since I was such an "athlete," I assumed that I would be out in front, running across the finish line, feeling victorious. The reality was that I did the run a few seconds faster each day, but with a lot of effort and struggle to take just a few seconds off my time.

One morning at 5:00 a.m., I woke up to a horrendous pain. Somehow in my sleep I had gotten a charley horse and had pulled a calf muscle in the process. I stumbled out of bed, upset over what I was going to do about the morning run. How could I tell the "powers that be"—oh, my God!—that I couldn't do it! I felt humiliated and embarrassed, like a failure. I hobbled to the doctor on site to see if a miracle could be performed within the next thirty minutes before the run that would cure me of my affliction. The doctor didn't seem to think the world had ended, as I did, and said it was up to me to deal with the situation however I wanted. He was so EST! I went around to some of the "powers that be" to get sympathy, advice, and encouragement, or to find someone who would tell me to buck up, take it, and just get out there and stop whining. Everyone said the same thing—it's up to me whether or not I wanted to run or to sit it out. Sit it out! Sit it out!? How could I just sit it out?

At the appointed time, after much physical and mental agony, I hobbled up to the starting line to join the others for the last day of the run. For some reason there was at least some part of me that was sane. I gave myself permission to be gentle with myself. I allowed myself to take it easy, to just enjoy it, to simply do it. I didn't push, I didn't "try." I just wanted to start the run and see if I could finish it. It was also okay to stop if I was in any kind of pain. During the run I kept a pretty slow and steady pace, favored my bad leg, and kept on going. Since I was moving slower I noticed the scenery more, enjoyed some great talks with the other "limpers," and had a great time.

As I crossed the finish line I knew that my time would be at least five minutes slower than the time I had been desperately trying to beat each day. When the timekeeper yelled out, "Karen Drucker: 10:05," I stopped dead in my tracks. "You must have made a mistake!" I practically yelled at him. Each day I had been doing the run in 10:45, running full out, efforting, sweating, trying. "Are you sure about this time?" He showed me the stopwatch. He was right, and a huge life lesson was learned. I didn't "try," I just did it, enjoyed it, and wound up easily and effortlessly accomplishing the goal.

Many years have passed since that experience, but I still remember it. When I am stressed or feeling pressured, I try to remember to ask myself if I am trying too hard. If I am, I remember the lesson of the daily run. It always helps me to remember to be gentle with myself.

"Self care is never a selfish act - it is simply good stewardship of the only gift that I have." — PARKER PALMER

Gentle with Myself

Words & Music: Karen Drucker
Chorus words: Robyn Posin

I will be gentle with myself.
I will be gentle with myself.
I will hold myself like a newborn baby child.

I will be tender with my heart.
I will be tender with my heart.
I will hold my heart like a newborn baby child.

CHORUS:
I will only go as fast as the slowest part of me feels safe to go.

I will be easy on myself.
I will be easy on myself.
I love myself like a newborn baby child.

CHORUS:
I will only go as fast as the slowest part of me feels safe to go.

I am gentle with myself.
I am gentle with myself.
I hold myself like a newborn baby child.
I rock myself like a newborn baby child.
I love myself like a newborn baby child.

CHAPTER 25

In Beauty May I Walk

I am a woman who walks. I walk for my body, but much more so for my head. An hour of walking and being with my thoughts has been better for me than all of the therapy money can buy.

I walk alone on the mountain near my home, or along the water by the San Francisco Bay, or in the woods near my house. When I travel to different cities for work, I often get to my hotel room, dump my bags, and immediately take off to discover where I am by walking.

I walk early in the morning before anyone is up. Some days I walk down the mountain into town for a morning latte. On other days, I walk on a trail right outside my front door. I am blessed to live in a place where there is a hiking trail near my house. A few times a week I walk a trail that winds through the woods, amid the sound of water trickling down the hills and the fragrance of bay trees. I end up at the top of a hill that has become my prayer spot. With endorphins pumping, and the wind from the ocean in the distance on my face, I say thanks and send my prayers over the mountains for the world and for my friends, and simply give thanks.

I always walk with a little pouch around my waist that has paper and a pen in it. Maybe it's because I am in nature and away from any distractions, but here is where I "hear" Spirit. I constantly stop and write down ideas, song lyrics, anything that is on my mind. Even now, I am typing these words that I wrote from this morning's walk. I have come up with more song ideas by taking a walk than I ever have from sitting at a piano.

I walk with my husband. At least once a week, we walk in a park that has giant redwood trees. We get there right before closing so that the park is nearly empty. It almost feels like you can hear the giant redwoods talk to you, and the music of the stream running through the park is a soothing backdrop. We stretch out on the benches and stare up at the trees that tower over 250 feet high, and just lie there in silence.

On Thanksgiving and Christmas we do our annual hike to the top of Mt. Tamalpais where there is a 360° view of the Bay Area. It's 2,571 feet to the top, and we hike there in about three hours. We have done this hike in the rain, in fog, with winds, no matter what. Every year. The endorphin rush is amazing, and the fact that we can eat a wonderful fattening holiday meal with no guilt (well, almost) makes it all worth it.

I have walked the famous Dipsea stairs in Mill Valley for the Escape from Alcatraz Triathlon. After swimming from Alcatraz to San Francisco and biking from San Francisco to Mill Valley, I then walked from Mill Valley over the mountain to Stinson Beach and back—14 miles total, up and over the mountain. I can't say I was walking at the finish line. It was more like hobbling and limping.

My love of walking led me to participate in the Avon Breast Cancer walk from Santa Barbara, California, to Los Angeles, in memory of my mother and others fighting breast cancer. When I signed up, I raised the pledge money and trained daily but had no idea what I was in for. The walk was twenty miles a day for three days, walking, talking, whining, connecting with amazing women, and being inspired. I walked, and walked, and walked, and swore I would never walk long distances again. I was back walking within a week.

I walk, but I do not run. I used to run years ago, but then I discovered walking. Besides, whenever I see runners they look so miserable and intense, not like they are having a lot of fun. I want fun, so I walk.

I walk because I don't think of it as exercise. I think of people who say they hate to exercise and just wish they could know the feeling of oneness and serenity that you can feel after a walk.

I walk because it makes me feel connected: to nature, to myself, to Spirit. I walk because I love it. So I gotta go—gotta go walk.

"In every walk with nature one receives far more than he seeks."
JOHN MUIR

In Beauty May I Walk

Words: adapted by Karen Drucker
Music: Karen Drucker

BASED ON THE NAVAJO POEM:
"IN BEAUTY MAY I WALK"

In beauty, may I walk.
All day long, may I walk.
Through the seasons, may I walk.
May I walk in peace. May I walk in peace.

On this path, may I walk.
Through my life, may I walk.
In old age, may I walk.
May I walk in peace. May I walk in peace.

CHORUS:
May I walk. May I walk. May I walk in peace. (Repeat)

In joy, may I walk.
In love, may I walk.
In gratitude, may I walk.
May I walk in peace. May I walk in peace.

In stillness, may I walk.
In forgiveness, may I walk.
In loving kindness, may I walk.
May I walk in peace. May I walk in peace.

CHORUS

Lighten Up

It is every performer's dream to have a standing ovation at the end of a performance, to look out on the mass of faces and to see everyone smiling, whooping it up, and applauding madly. For you! It is the ultimate validation to know that you have moved them, touched them, done something that made them want to get up from their chairs and give something back to you.

So there I was, after performing a ninety-minute concert to a wonderful group of people, looking like I was basking in the glow of all that love, but where was I? Where was I really? I was checked out. I looked like I was taking it all in and being grateful, but actually, on that particular night, it was, I must confess, an act. As I was on stage smiling and taking my bows, a voice inside was raging in my brain saying, "What are you doing? Why are you not feeling this? You must be really messed up! You have worked for years to get to this point, and now you want to be somewhere else? What is your problem? You are so ungrateful!" The truth was, I was simply tired. I had been saying yes to every job opportunity that came in and traveling the country like a traveling salesman. I thought I was "being in service," but in reality my flame was flickering and the pilot light was about to go out. I wanted to just go back to my hotel room, take a nice hot shower, order something fattening from room service, and watch a movie. What happened?

The experience that night got my attention, and I realized I needed to do something about it.

I heard about a class starting in my area called "Awakening Joy." It was be a one-year, once a month class of looking at the word "joy." Even though the class sounded perfect for what was going on with me, I was amazed at my resistance to making a commitment to it. However, the seed was planted and I started to become aware of how much joy, or lack of joy, was in my life. I decided that I had to work through my resistance and just sign up.

Once a month about 200 of us would cram into a church in Berkeley, California, and hear discussions, songs, and people's stories all about what the experience of joy is.

In my monthly classes I learned that joy comes in many shapes, sizes, and expressions. I realized that joy is like that expression, "One person's trash is another person's treasure." What brings me joy might be boring or painful to someone else. For example, I love cleaning, vacuuming and organizing, while others might think that was their version of hell. I discovered that I needed to get in touch with what really brings my heart joy, so I started making a list: Being home, puttering and organizing, laughing, planting flowers, swimming in the bay, having days with no plans or time agendas, being with my hubby, being with friends, playing with my cats, seeing movies, going out to eat, getting a massage, taking long walks, being creative, and the list went on.

It soon became clear to me that I didn't often allow myself time to do a lot of these things. The inner driver in my head kept me chained to the computer for hours doing boring business tasks. I wasn't taking the time to give myself what would really bring me joy.

To change this, I started small. I started making "joy" dates with myself. Like a spiritual practice, I chose to notice daily what brought me joy as well as what felt soul draining. My friend, author Alan Cohen, has an exercise that illustrates this perfectly. You look at something (or someone) and simply notice if it "Is It" or "Not It," if it is "A Match" or "Not a Match." If something "Is It," you feel excited, vibrant, and alive, while the "Not It" makes you feel drained, lethargic, and bored. I started looking at different situations, things I was doing, even people I would encounter, and see if it was a match or not a match. Did I feel alive and happy, or drained and feeling like I wanted to run for the hills?

I kept this up for a while and noticed that my level of being "present" was returning, my energy was up, and my joy meter was rising. I had lightened up about everything and was just having more fun. I was enjoying performing again, feeling excited about new projects, and experiencing gratitude for everything in my life.

And the joy class? I kept it up for a while, until I realized that my joy was right there inside of me, available at every moment. I just needed to choose joy and lighten up. I didn't need to go to a class anymore to find it.

"Blessed are we who can laugh at ourselves for we shall never cease to be amused." — UNKNOWN

Lighten Up

Words: Karen Drucker
Music: Karen Drucker & John Hoy

I was walkin' down the street, I was feelin' mighty fine,
'Till I caught a glimpse in a window of my behind.
There was a jiggle and a wiggle that I'd never seen before.
And as I looked a little closer Oh my God I found more!
I freaked out and I shrieked out "This has just ruined my day!"
'Till I heard a voice inside me say ...

CHORUS:
Lighten Up, don't take it so seriously.
Lighten Up, trust the mystery.
Lighten Up, it doesn't matter anyway.
Just enjoy your life and get out of your way. Lighten Up!

So now I'm headed to a party to meet my friends.
I've got an outfit that's to die for — Honey I am just the
    living end!
But as I scope out the scene it's obvious to me,
that the money at this party is simply obscene.
They're talking about their mansions, their yachts,
and dropping names,
and in an instant I feel unworthy, small and ashamed.
But as I try to make a beeline, slip out the back door,
I hear that voice inside me saying once more ...

CHORUS

Worrying and judging, what good does it do?
When you compare yourself to me and I compare myself to you?
This disease to please has just got to go.
When I love myself that's all I need to know.

So now I'm looking in the mirror and a new wrinkle has appeared.
Do I curse? Do I stress? It's the thing I most feared.
But then I remember my new mantra and I soon realize,
that I am perfect even with wrinkles and cellulite thighs.
I don't have to change a thing, struggle or try,
'cause my real beauty comes from deep inside...

CHORUS:
Lighten Up, don't take it so seriously.
Lighten Up, trust the mystery.
Lighten Up, it doesn't matter anyway.
Just enjoy your life and get out of your way. Lighten Up!

CHAPTER 27

Let Go of the Shore

"Clarity is the state of seeing clearly, seeing things in a new light, like applying Windex to your soul." — CHERIE CARTER-SCOTT

He put the key in the lock of his basement door, turned it, and with a deep breath opened up the door. This friend of mine, this spiritual seeker, this person who is always digging deep into his soul to discover new parts of himself and grow, had confessed to me about the dark place in his life where he just refused to go: his basement. This was his big secret. No one knew about the clutter that lived in his basement and no one ever got to see it.

That didn't make sense to me. How could someone be so devoted to a spiritual path, yet have clutter and chaos at the root of his physical surroundings?

When I was first starting out as a singer, I had many odd jobs, but one of my favorites was being a professional organizer. It was heaven for me to come into someone's cluttered garage, and just a few hours later have it be clean, organized, and looking like a brand-new room. My clients would "ooh" and "ah," I would feel fulfilled like I had really made a difference in their lives, and I would move on to the next client. A funny thing happened, though. I began to notice that about two weeks after I had swooped in and cleared everything out for them, it would be back to where it had been— totally disorganized. I finally realized after many experiences of organizing and reorganizing people that there was more to this subject than just organizing the stuff or throwing it away. I began to ask people specifically about their clutter. What was it that they were moving around or throwing away? What were these items and what did they mean to them? That's when I got it. As with so many things in life, cleaning the clutter wasn't really about the clutter. It was about the belief underneath all the "stuff."

I talked about this at length with my friend, about how clearing out the clutter in our physical, mental and spiritual lives could affect everything we do. We talked about how it could put closure on relationships that have never been healed, motivate us to take better care of our health, or help us to gain clarity about the dreams we have not yet realized.

We talked about the basements, attics, and garages filled with old books and "mystery" papers from our past, the closets filled with old clothes that no longer fit who we are now. All of these things live on, gathering dust around our psychic soul.

Our discussion went a little deeper, going into the beliefs and the fears about what it would be like to have space. What was he really letting go of and what would happen if he released, surrendered, let go? The main question we kept asking was this: If you let that (book, picture, letter—fill in the blank) go, what will be in its place?

I have found that when I talk to people about these deeper levels, the concept of "empty space" comes up. Some people are thrilled by it; others are terrified. Some think that the space feels like freedom, while others want to fill the space immediately with something new, like filling up silence with chattering talk.

The more I thought about it, the more I realized that life has many births and deaths, literally and spiritually. These births and deaths involve letting go of the shore that we have known and setting sail into new, unknown, uncharted waters. Ultimately, to do this means trusting that we are okay, that we have what we need, and that we are safe.

Our "stuff" symbolizes for us a place or persona that we identified with at a previous point in our lives. Pictures, letters, books, and clothes can bring us right back to that period of time. Sometimes it is wonderful to go down memory lane and be swept up in wonderfully rich memories and emotions. But sometimes that stuff is what is holding us back, keeping us stuck, acting as weights on our feet. How can we move forward on our spiritual path when we have not allowed those old parts of us (the old job, relationship, or self-image) to die so we can be reborn onto the new path that Spirit is asking us to travel?

It is a challenging spiritual practice to keep "uncluttered" in this way. I have agonized over throwing books away until I realized their subject matter related to where I was then, not now, and it was time for me to release them. I realized that whenever I looked at my bookshelf and saw those books that represented my old "issues," I would mentally go back to that time in my life. Why not celebrate that I have healed that part of myself and give the books away to those who could benefit from the information?

As I was writing this, I thought about my professional wardrobe and wondered if there were things I needed to let go of. I just finished a new mission statement in which I set my intention this year to perform at conferences as a singer and as a speaker. I had to laugh when I looked in my closet and saw that most of my "performing clothes" were from my years as a wedding singer. They were all in great shape but clearly nothing I would want to wear onstage now in this new incarnation as a speaker. I carefully took each of the sequined dresses and black tux-like suits out of my closet, agonizing over getting rid of them. However, I realized that even though they were in fine shape, they had the energy of "wedding singer" all over them. For example, I looked at one outfit and instantly remembered the mother of the bride yelling at me for not playing enough polkas at her daughter's wedding! Clearly these clothes had to go in order to make room for whatever my new look would be as "the new me." When I thought about someone else wearing them and getting benefit from them, it was easier to let them all go.

I went through the same mental gymnastics over my everyday clothes that I haven't worn in a year and the paperwork from old jobs that are done and gone. I have found for me it's not about throwing it all away. The truth is I am a sentimental sap and love saving things. The difference now is that I simply have a limit to how much I keep. I have one big box for letters, one bookcase for my books, and one big Rubbermaid bin for miscellaneous mementos. I have made a rule with myself that when I get something new, I have to throw out something old. It's about being conscious and aware of when something is dying or "dead" in my life, and recognizing that this is about so much more than possessions. I have had to mentally cut the cords of certain relationships so they could die or, if they were meant to continue, they could be born anew. I have had to get quiet enough to hear that still, small voice inside whisper to my soul, "You're done," after realizing it was time to leave a relationship, move from where I was living, or leave a job that I had simply outgrown. For me, it's all about making the choice to separate from the old and move on so I don't have cobwebs in my mind.

I have had many labels in my life, identifying the various ages and stages I have gone through. I have been known as a struggling musician, wedding singer, music teacher, housecleaner, and girlfriend, to name a few. I had to let many of these labels of identification "die" so that new ones could be born, and part of shedding the old was to also let go of some of the symbols and "stuff" that identified me with these labels. In this way, I could make space for the "new me" to emerge with new identities like recording artist, workshop leader, writer, speaker, wife.

This is my path. It is a constant process of surrendering to what is, what is next, who I am, what is emerging, and what needs to be released. It is about letting go of the safety of the shore and of what I have known, and floating into the mystery that is this amazing life.

So, what's in your basement?

"One doesn't discover new lands without consenting to
lose sight of the shore." — ANDRÉ GIDE

Let Go of the Shore

Words & Music: Karen Drucker

CHORUS:
Let go of the shore,
and let the water carry you.
Let go of the shore,
float into the mystery. (Repeat)

You have all you need,
it's all inside of you.
Close your eyes and breathe,
and know that you are safe.

CHORUS

No need to make a plan,
your heart will be your compass.
Just lift your sails in faith,
and trust that you will arrive.

CHORUS

**Part Three:
Let It Shine**

CHAPTER 28

What Would Love Do?

Everyone deals with adversity differently. In my father's case, he tried to kill himself.

My dad was a force of nature. Funny, commanding, sensitive, the life of the party, impatient, and very controlling, he could walk into a room and simply take over with his laugh-a-minute stories and pure joie de vivre. People either loved him or hated him, and he didn't really care either way. He lived the way he wanted, and that was that. He had built a life by leaving Brooklyn, New York, and coming to Beverly Hills, California, in the 1940's. He became a comedy writer for radio, and later on, a publisher of small trade magazines for the fashion industry and for dog breeders. He then "retired" with a self-created business of taking people on tennis tours around the world, where they would sightsee and play tennis all day long. He had his home in the Hollywood Hills, swam and played tennis religiously at his beloved tennis club, and drove to his office in the early morning with the top down on his convertible, blaring Frank Sinatra big band records from his eight-track player and singing at the top of his lungs. He loved life and lived it to the fullest.

When he was diagnosed with prostate cancer in his late 60's, he didn't take it well. This did not fit into his plan, although his father had died of the same disease at around the same age. My dad was physically fit and would never even take an aspirin. I think he was in denial that anything bad could ever happen to him. He kept the cancer a secret from my mother for a couple of years (how he did that still amazes me) and then swore her to secrecy to keep it from my sister and me. The stress of holding that information for the next few years must have been tremendous on my mother, but somehow she did it.

After operations and treatments and a long fight with the cancer, our parents realized that it was time to tell my sister and me, so we could finally, as a family, deal with it. My dad's condition was definitely deteriorating and he had to stop the activities that had been his lifeblood—playing tennis and swimming. The medication he was on left him listless and bloated, sucking all the life force out of him. He was losing his independence, and he could see where this path was leading. He hated it and he wanted no part of it.

At this point in my life, I was singing in nightclubs and at private parties, and flying home whenever I could to spend time with him. When he called and asked me to fly down to Los Angeles to take my mom out for a special night at the theater, I flew down the following weekend.

I took my mom out for the evening and we had a great time. When we came home, my dad was in bed where we had left him four hours earlier, but now there was this funny breathing we heard. I realized in that moment it was the "death rattle" that occurs when people are in the process of dying and their breathing becomes labored. Then we saw the empty pillbox on the nightstand. We called 911, and it seemed like it took an eternity for the ambulance to get there as we listened to the long mournful siren coming up the canyon. My father was taken to UCLA Medical Center where, after a team worked on him, he was saved.

He was not pleased. When we came into his hospital room he was angry and humiliated. How were we going to get through this? It felt overwhelming and impossible. We had aborted his grand plan and now we had "forced" him to deal with the reality of what had just happened—as well as the fact that he was dying.

His doctor immediately took him off the medication he had been on, and the result was amazing. Instantly, his personality came back and it was clear that a lot of his depression and the suicide attempt was a result of his medication not working properly.

He was definitely declining physically, but the miracle that we had hoped for occurred. He was open to the idea of having us all go through this together as a family, realizing that he was not alone and that we would stand by him.

For most of my childhood my father had been very critical and demanding of me. Thinking that praising me would lead to a swelled head, his style of parenting was always to keep the carrot dangling in front of me, making me try harder to get his approval. Of course, nothing I did was ever good enough and I would try harder, work longer, and strive for that ever-elusive seal of approval. I will never forget when he saw me perform at a big corporate convention with my band. While my mom gushed about how good I was, he kept telling me that I really should become a party planner. He told me that my real talent was being a producer, being behind the scenes, not up on stage. (Thank God for years of therapy and for following what was in my heart instead of doing what he wanted me to do.)

Now off the medication and coming to terms with what he had done, the side of his personality that was impatient, demanding, and controlling was gone. Emerging in its place was the sweet, sentimental, gentle side of him that I loved being with. For the forty years my parents had lived in our house, I had never seen him sit outside and just "be" in the garden. Now that was what he did all day long. I would see him sitting there in the afternoon just silently holding hands with my mother. Often I would sit with him and he would marvel at all of the birds that would splash around in the birdbath, or talk about the beauty of the flowers, or just sit in silence with a sweet expression on his face. He was astounded that he had never really seen the beauty that had been here all along. He would tell me stories for hours, ones I had heard a hundred times before about old Hollywood, his travels around the globe, or his philosophy of life. I would gobble up everything he was saying like an eager student trying to gain as much wisdom before the Master moves on. We laughed together, cried together, held each other, and bonded more in those six months than we ever had in my whole life.

When the time came and he knew he didn't have much time left, he decided he wanted to go to the hospital instead of dying at home. I think in that last selfless act he did for my mother, he realized that having nurses, strangers, and medical equipment in our house would be a hard memory for her to live with. We gingerly put him in the car and, in silence, drove him to the hospital.

By now my sister had joined us and we would make the pilgrimage every day from our home in Hollywood to Cedars-Sinai Medical Center in Beverly Hills to be with him. At this point he was not able to speak, and I had a big internal laugh the morning when we walked in and he pointed to the imaginary watch on his wrist, with a look of frustration on his face. I just knew he was saying, "Okay, I made the decision that I was ready to go. Why the hell is it taking so long!?" I learned that even up until the last moments of your life, if you are impatient or have control issues, they will still be there!

My father passed peacefully on July 31, 1991. Interestingly enough, we had all been in the room with him that day, surrounding him with love. Around 5:00 p.m., with his condition not changing, we made the decision to go home. Around 8:00 p.m., I felt a strong urge to go back to the hospital. My mom and sister were tired and said they would go back in the morning, but I couldn't let the feeling go. I went back to the hospital and, sure enough, there was that same hard breathing sound I had heard six months earlier. This time he was leaving, and this time I was with him.

During this challenging time, I had been reading Stephen Levine's wonderful book about the death process, *Meetings at the Edge*. The book gave me techniques to deal with an experience I was finding so unfamiliar and so scary. There was one technique I practiced daily. Every time I felt my heart constrict from fear, I would breathe deeply and visualize my heart opening and softening. This would help me to gently bring myself back to the situation and be present. I would just keep focusing on love and keep breathing. Every time I opened the door to my

Dad's hospital room, I would have to remember this technique. I would have to consciously breathe and soften my heart because I would immediately want to run away and hide. And now, in this moment of being with him in his final hours, I felt like this was some kind of divine plan in which I was supposed to be the only one with him at the end.

I sat with him in that dark, gray hospital room and prayed, sang quietly to him, and thanked him a final time for all of the love and lessons he had given me. I promised him I would make the most of my life and told him I hoped he would always be proud of the woman I had become and the woman I was becoming.

Murray Donald Drucker
September 3, 1919 - July 31, 1991

"Life is no brief candle to me. It is a sort of splendid torch which I have got hold of for the moment, and I want to make it burn as brightly as possible before handing it on to future generations."
GEORGE BERNARD SHAW

What Would Love Do?

Words: Karen Drucker
Music: Karen Drucker & John Hoy

Whenever I have hurt in my heart I ask, what would love do?
Whenever I don't know where to turn I ask, what would love do?
Whenever I don't know what to say I ask, what would love do?
What would love do? What would love do?

Anytime that I am stuck in my pain I ask, what would love do?
Anytime that I feel ashamed I ask, what would love do?
Anytime I can't find my truth I ask, what would love do?
What would love do? What would love do?

CHORUS:
Love has all the answers.
Love makes no demands.
Love will lead me to the truth,
and help me to understand that life is all about love.

When I have something hard I need to say I ask, what would love do?
When it seems another block is in my way I ask, what would love do?
When it seems I can't face another day I ask, what would love do?
What would love do? What would love do?

CHORUS

In any situation I ask, what would love do?
When I'm feeling limitation I ask, what would love do?
I have to look into my soul and ask, what would love do?
What would love do? What would love do?

CHAPTER 29

I Am Healed

I guess I didn't have a choice about it. It happened before I was six years old. I was signed up and committed before I even had the idea that this would be a lifelong relationship that I would never leave. And yet as time moved on, this relationship grew deeper and sweeter, and it eventually would become a haven and sanctuary whenever I needed it, although there were years of resentment, yelling, and stubbornness.

I am a swimmer, and my relationship with water is one I will always value and cherish.

My father was a competitive swimmer in college at the University of North Carolina, Chapel Hill. He so loved his memories of being captain of his swim team that my sister and I were immediately put on a team as soon as we could swim the length of the pool. By the age of six, I had started a routine that would continue all through my school years. Workouts every day for two hours after school, including a thirty-minute drive to the team pool, then weekend swim meets all over Southern California. We would swim, rain or shine, sick or well. My life revolved around what big meet was coming up that I was training for, as well as all of the dramas of my teammates. I felt the pain of self-consciousness when I developed breasts at eleven years old (no one else had yet) and had to stand on the blocks in my skintight Speedo tank suit in front of the boys on my team. It only got worse in high school. I would often work out with the boys' team and they would be at the bottom of the pool with their goggles looking up, pointing and laughing as I swam by.

This routine got harder as my "normal" friends were going

to movies, hanging out at the mall and being typical teenagers, while I was always going off to workouts. There were times when I would see friends coming home from the movies and they would say, "Oh, we didn't think to call you. We just assumed you were swimming." My friends wound up being my fellow swimmers and we would all suffer from the same anxieties of making our coach unhappy, doing badly in a meet, or trying to be winners.

I could see how I adapted to this last fact, when after years of having all of my swimming medals stuck in a shoebox, I finally honored those years of competition and had my medals put into a beautiful velvet-backed frame. It was no accident that they formed a perfect triangle with a few blue first-places, more red second-places, and yet even more white third-places. You always wanted to at least get a third place because you would get a medal. If you got fourth place, you would just get a wimpy ribbon. In seeing this triangle of blue, red, and white medals, I realized this manifested into my role with my swimming friends. I really wasn't all that comfortable being the winner. I was content to let them win and I would place second or third.

My relationship with the water took a dramatic turn when I left high school. We were done, over, finished. If I never looked at a pool again it would not be too soon. I had spent years in this relationship, and I was over it. I wanted to be normal and to have pizza dates with friends, not smell like chlorine and have no social life. So we broke up. I went off to college and never looked back.

Then in my mid-twenties, a phone call changed it all. I had just gotten dumped by a boyfriend and was having daily pity parties for myself, when my sister came to the rescue. She suggested that I check out the local high school pool and join an adult swim program. She thought swimming for fun might help my mood. From that first lap it all came rushing back: the feeling of freedom, the sheer joy of moving through the water, the effortlessness, the ease, the timeless sensation of flowing. At a time in my life where it felt like everything was a struggle, swimming was the one place where I could just let go and surrender. My affair with the water was back on track. I joined an adult masters swim team, then an open water team, and had a whole new social life with swimmers who just wanted to be healthy and have fun. What a concept!

One day when my father was in the last few months of his life, dealing with his terminal cancer, I suggested we go for a swim. He thought I was nuts, but his face lit up. Though he was barely walking and looked weak and frail, he agreed to go. We drove to our nearby club pool and I helped him into the water. Within seconds he was doing his familiar freestyle stroke. Although he was moving very slowly, he was able to swim laps with me. I will never forget the sweet way he looked at me when we got to the wall and he said, "Thank you for bringing me here." We pushed off the wall and I swam stroke for stroke with him with tears clouding up my goggles. My father had introduced me to his love of the water and now it was my turn to repay him.

Ernest Holmes says: "To be immersed in water symbolizes our recognition that we are surrounded by pure Spirit. It is the outward sign of an inner conviction." I ran across another quotation recently that to me says the same thing in different words: "Swimming: From the outside looking in, you can't understand it. From the inside looking out, you can't explain it." I truly can't explain the feeling of freedom, and how I am healed every time I am in the water, knowing this affair will go on forever.

"Healing may not be so much about getting better, as about letting go of everything that isn't you - all of the expectations, all of the beliefs -and becoming who you are." — RACHEL NAOMI REMEN

I Am Healed

Words & Music: Karen Drucker & Kate Munger

(With each verse, substitute the 1st, 2nd & 4th line. In the last verse you will *send* the healing power instead of *call*.)

UP FROM MY FEET, I call the healing power.
UP FROM MY FEET, I draw it to my heart.
It's already here, I only need to claim it.
UP FROM MY FEET, I know that I am healed.

IN THROUGH MY HANDS, I call the healing power.
IN THROUGH MY HANDS, I draw it to my heart.
It's already here, I only need to claim it.
IN THROUGH MY HANDS, I know that I am healed

DOWN FROM MY HEAD, I call the healing power.

WITH MY SPIRIT AND SOUL, I call the healing power.

UP FROM THE EARTH, I call the healing power.

BACK TO THE EARTH, I send the healing power.

CHAPTER 30

Feel It

"We are what we repeatedly do." — ARISTOTLE

Most of my friends think I am nuts. When I tell people what my hobby is, what brings me the most joy, what is the most spiritual act that I do, they look at me like I am crazy. Maybe I am, but that's too bad because I don't plan to stop. I swim in the San Francisco Bay.

It all started when I was asked to be on a relay team swimming across Lake Tahoe. I had aspired to be in the Olympics as a kid, and trained by swimming two to four hours a day, but I never achieved the star status required to make it to that high level. I swam at a national competition level until I was about sixteen, and then gave it up for swimming on my Hollywood High School team. About eight years later I found Masters Swimming and joined a team.

Being an adult without the need of parental approval and no longer having coaches yelling at me, I dove right in (pardon the reference) and loved the workouts, the camaraderie, and the feeling of doing something I could do easily and effortlessly. When

I was asked to be part of a relay team of six women swimming across Lake Tahoe, where each of us would swim for thirty minutes at a time until we completed the fifteen-mile swim, I was scared and excited. A teammate suggested that I "try not to panic too much" when I jumped into the 57-degree water and was gasping for breath. Six hours later, standing on the other side of the lake and looking back at where we had started, I felt a thrill that pool swimming could never give me. I was hooked.

I had seen some crazy people swimming in Aquatic Park at Ghirardelli Square in San Francisco and had heard they did an annual swim in San Francisco Bay from "The Rock," or Alcatraz Island. I found out that these crazy people belonged to something called the Dolphin Club, which was an old, funky blue building that has been there since 1877. Sitting right at the end of Hyde Street, where the cable cars end, the Dolphin Club has only allowed women to join the club since 1976. I walked into the building, with its antique rowboats and pictures on the walls of the lifetime members, and knew I had come "home."

I immediately joined and began training for what would be my first open water solo swim. I will never forget the thrill of swimming from Alcatraz to San Francisco. Early one fall morning, before the Bay got crowded with sailboats, a ferry boat took about sixty members from the club across the Bay to Alcatraz. I dove from the boat, swam to the shore, then stole a pebble from the beach and stuck it in my suit to prove I had actually been there. The boat sounded the starting horn and we were off, swimming the mile and a half back to the club. When I was done, being able to look across the Bay and know I had accomplished the swim was an empowering feeling. The next day, I was amazed at how cold the water felt and swore that it must have dropped five degrees overnight. It was my first lesson in what focus and intention does to you, mentally. The water temperature had not dropped, but I had been so focused on accomplishing my goal that I had not noticed the cold temperature. Now I could feel how cold that water actually was.

For me, the spiritual aspect of swimming in the Bay is a daily practice. The water is cold. It can range to the high 40's in the winter to the low 60's in the summer. The process of hitting that initial wall of cold is never easy, and it never feels warm. I have been known to swear like a sailor on particularly cold days. I look at that first shock as a metaphor for my life. How often do I come up against something that is hard, or that feels like a portal I have to move through, and I have a decision to make of moving through it or backing away. I see plenty of people get in up to their knees and then turn away and run back to the shore. I have done this plenty of times myself! But I found the trick is to just breathe and actually embrace the cold, flow with it, surrender into it, then suddenly the body responds and I move into a whole other world. The sounds, the smells, the way my skin feels against the cold, it all adds up to this magical place that only few enter.

There is actually a word in the dictionary for all of this: "curglaff: n. the shock felt on plunging into cold water."

A lot of people asks the question, "What about sharks?" The truth is that the San Francisco Bay is too cold for sharks. There might be what they call Bay Sharks that are small and swim at the bottom of the Bay, but they are not the kind of shark that would hurt people. It's the seals that concern me. There are a lot of them out there, and every once in a while you see them pop their little heads up, look around, and disappear again into the dark water. For me, this is another life metaphor: I can allow myself to look down into the murk where I can't really see anything and let my imagination run wild with what could be there, or I can focus on keeping my head up, looking around at the beauty, and keeping my attention on the joy I am feeling. I always laugh at the times when I am just about to enter the water and some seal pops up right in my line of sight. What a practice of letting go and trusting and just enjoying my swim, as opposed to thinking every moment of some imaginary thing that could happen to me. By the way, for the most part the seals are harmless. If anything, they want to play and might tap your feet.

The Dolphin Club has been my sanctuary. I love everything about it, from the people, who are some of the most interesting people I have ever met, to the funky building with its pictures, smells and history. Then there are the old, leathery-skinned men who sit in the sun all day. They have their routine of a short swim followed by their daily bourbon, and then spend the afternoon just watching the women coming out of the water. It all adds up to the most colorful place that I know.

I remember the afternoon that I flew home from Los Angeles, emotionally raw from having just come from my father's funeral a few days before. As if my car had a mind of its own, it steered me right to the front of the club. Feeling as if I was cleansing my soul in that cold water, I remember swimming and crying and coming out of the water like I had released something from myself. I felt about ten pounds lighter, emotionally.

So year after year I swim. The Dolphin Club has a big wooden sign that is placed right at the door at the entryway to the water. It reads:

"Renew thyself completely each day.
Do it again and again and forever again."

And so I do, and so I will....

"The best and most beautiful things in the world cannot be seen, nor touched...but are felt in the heart." — HELEN KELLER

Feel It

Words: Karen Drucker
Music: Karen Drucker & John Hoy

INTRO:
I'm gonna' just feel it and let it be.
Allow my feelings to come naturally.
Moving through me like clouds in the sky,
I don't question why, I'm gonna just feel it.

   CHORUS:
   Feel it. I'm gonna' let the joy and pain wash over me.
   Feel it. I'm gonna' ride the waves and let it be.
   Feel it. I'm gonna' trust it'll be ok to let it flow.
   Feel it. I'm gonna' laugh and cry and let it go.

I've spent so many years trying to push my pain away,
but I know that what I resist persists and can surface any day.
So I'm taking the steps to see what I've denied,
I'll open to the feelings I've held deep inside.
I'm open. I'm willing. I am ready to...

   CHORUS

Being strong shouldn't mean that I'm not supposed to feel.
Tell me how do I grow? How can I heal?
I've got to let it out, let it all come through,
every kind of emotion, what I've got to do,
is be open, and willing, and ready to ...

   CHORUS

CHAPTER 31

Three Little Words

I was desperately trying to keep up with Monica at swim practice today. She is a lean, mean, and driven triathlon machine. I work out with these super athletes who do triathlons, and their dedication and resilience is inspiring. I have done a few triathlons in my life, but the amount of time that it takes to train on each sport was too much for me. However, Monica, a mother of two, loves doing triathlons and trains daily for them.

At the end of a hard swim set as we were huffing and puffing, she mentioned to all of us in her lane that this weekend she was signed up for a long, hard triathlon that she was really nervous about. As if it were a rehearsed scene with everyone saying their memorized lines from a script, those of us who had done this particular race chimed in with our two cents' worth. Steve went on about how hard it was and about that awful steep hill at the end. Dave mentioned the heat. Lynn talked about the sheer will and endurance it would require. As we pushed off for our next set, all I could think about was how perfectly the law of attraction works. Monica had said she was nervous, and as if on cue the Universe supported her thought and gave more evidence to prove her right. I thought about how, in the world of athletics (and in life), you train your body to be able to accomplish a goal, and yet how much time is spent on training your mind as well? Monica's mental idea of what this event would be like is just as important as how well physically she trains for it.

There are many studies that have proven that mental visualization is as important as actually training for a sport. Jack Nicklaus, the world famous golfer, has said that he will not even pick up a club until he has a mental image in his mind of exactly how the ball will be hit, how it will fly through the air, where it will land on the ground, and then how it will go into the hole. He calls this technique "going to the movies," and it accounts for much of his success.

I have noticed that my most relaxed concerts have been when I mentally "rehearsed" before I ever hit the stage. It's as if I have already been there and I can see any problems before they happen. I have even written songs using the technique of mental rehearsal. I see and hear myself performing the song, and it eventually comes to be.

When Monica and I were in the locker room, I couldn't help but put my two cents in about her event. I asked her what kinds of things she had been saying to herself this week, and she replied with a long list of negative roadblocks that would surely sabotage her triathlon, or at least make the event a whole lot harder. I suggested that she didn't need to take on what everyone was saying about the triathlon. That was their own experience but it didn't have to be hers. She could have a totally different experience than any of them, and it would be uniquely her own. It could even be fun. She got it. She said that she would make it a practice this week to really listen and become conscious of everything she was saying to herself, and work on seeing this triathlon as a wonderful and exciting event. It was as if a light got turned on in her brain. She had been so focused on how hard this was going to be that there was no space for the idea that it actually could be fun.

Author Alan Cohen says in his book *A Deep Breath of Life*, "If you hold an image in mind long enough and feel it as real, you can manifest it...hold in mind images of the life you desire, and refuse to feed thoughts of what you do not wish. Watch your words."

Fast forward to the next week.....

I am once again desperately trying to keep up with Monica. She is one lean, mean, happy, triathlon queen. Her race was nothing like she had negatively been affirming. Yes, there were times when it was hard, but since she focused on what she wanted and had set the intention before she even started to have fun, enjoy herself, and simply finish, she felt great and was excited about her upcoming races. Now if only I could keep up with her!

"Watch your thoughts; they become words. Watch your words; they become actions. Watch your actions; they become habits. Watch your habits; they become character." — FRANK OUTLAW

Three Little Words

Words: Karen Drucker
Music: Karen Drucker & John Hoy

TITLE AND SONG CONCEPT INSPIRED BY
MARY MANIN MORRISSEY

I know three little words that can mean so much,
they give me power every day.
Three little words that can heal my life and
help me get out of my way.
Any time I hit a road block, this is what I say:

CHORUS:
Life is good. Let it go. Play full out. Yes I can.
Tell me more. I am blessed. Be here now. I love you.

I know the words that I say will determine
the way that my life is gonna' be.
When I say what I feel then I make it so real
to manifest my destiny.
I just think about what I'm sayin', that's the magic key.

CHORUS

When I trust my heart to say what's on my mind,
the truth will be revealed, it happens every time.
Words can heal my soul, words can help me through.
My words determine what I think and feel and do.

CHORUS

CHAPTER 32

Permission to Play

It was a perfect day for a swim. Well, not exactly a swim—more like a race. There were about fifty of us standing in our swimsuits, goggles in one hand, neoprene black caps in the other, waiting to swim in the San Francisco Bay under the Golden Gate Bridge. The Dolphin Club put on this race once a year, and I had swam it about five times before. The key to making it to the lighthouse on the other side of the bay was to keep looking up to make sure the bridge was right above you. The waves and the current are especially strong here, where the ocean meets the Bay, and it's definitely a challenging swim.

In the past I had usually finished within the top five swimmers, so I put pressure on myself to get out fast and keep my lead. How I had gotten into this competitive mode again was a mystery to me. When I quit swimming altogether after high school, I swore I would never compete again. The Masters Swim Team I worked out with was all about being social and having fun, and the Dolphin Club was just another extension of that. Maybe it was George who brought my competitive edge back to me. Every time I was on the shore waiting to swim in a race, he would challenge me, teasing me that this time I didn't have what it takes and that he would win. Sometimes I would win, and sometimes he would win. For this particular race I knew I had to breathe on both sides so I could keep him in my line of sight and also look up to make sure the bridge was above me, all the while being careful not to get swept back into the Bay by the strong currents.

We all heard the starting horn. We jumped in from the San Francisco side of the Bridge and starting swimming to the Marin County side. Within about five minutes the pack of swimmers had all spread out, and there was George, battling it out with me, stroke for stroke. Breathe to the right, breathe to the left, look to see where George is, put my head up to check for the Bridge, then do it all again.

We stayed this way for about fifteen minutes, until on my left breath, I noticed that George wasn't there. I stopped swimming and all of a sudden I saw his feet in the air. He was spinning around doing some kind of weird water ballet move. Was he doing a somersault in the Bay? He came back up for air and I said, "George what the heck are you doing? We're in a race here!" With the look of a ten-year-old boy on his face, he proceeded to do another somersault and pretended he was doing water ballet. Then he started splashing me and encouraging me to play with him. I was amazed, startled, and confused.

"Karen, tell me. How often are we underneath the Golden Gate Bridge? How often does anyone get to see a view like this? I am going to take the time to enjoy it!" It was a light bulb moment for me. This event that I had done so many times, that had been all about getting to the other side, winning or bettering my time, had robbed me of the thrill and adventure of what this experience actually was all about. I wondered how much I was missing in other areas of my life by literally burying my head down and just getting through it as opposed to savoring every delicious part of it.

I decided then to do my first somersault in the bay, and I actually did water ballet with George. Some of the other swimmers stopped and stared as if they thought we were nuts, and some joined us. Still others, who were thrilled that they would beat us, sped by hoping that victory was now theirs!

We eventually made it to the lighthouse, where we touched the rock with our hand. A person standing on the rock had the job of giving each of us a Popsicle stick with the number of the order in which we had come in written on it. We then swam to the waiting boat, climbed on, and reveled in our accomplishment. All of the top swimmers were drinking coffee and eating donuts, talking all about their strategies of the race. Was I in the top five? No. Did I care? No. Would I ever attempt being in the top five again? I thought not, since this had been the most fun I ever had in the Bay. I had given myself permission to play, and now I wanted more!

"Ever since happiness heard your name, it has been running through the streets trying to find you." — RUMI

Permission to Play

Words: Karen Drucker & Lisa Hammond
Music: Karen Drucker & John Hoy

I'm gonna dance with my shoes off, laugh with my friends.
Take time for me, ooh the fun never ends!
I enjoy my life, every day.
I deserve it and I claim it and I give myself permission to play.

CHORUS:
Permission to play! (Repeat)

The more I give to myself, the more that I have to give.
I commit to my joy, 'cause it's the only way to live.
I fill up my well, every day.
My priority is that I give myself permission to play.

CHORUS

BRIDGE:
I don't have to ask anybody, 'cause right now is my time!
I put myself first. I take care of me, and let my light shine!

I'm gonna live out loud, follow my heart.
Believe in my dreams, today I will start to take a risk, and let it be ok.
I deserve it and I claim it and I give myself permission to play.

CHORUS

CHAPTER 33

Life Goes On

"Be kinder than necessary, for everyone we meet is fighting some kind of battle." — AUTHOR UNKNOWN

I am always amazed at the resilience of the human spirit. We meet someone and carry on a conversation about the weather or the daily little peeves we both agree on, but beyond this superficial conversation there could be circumstances happening in the person's life that we know nothing about.

The Masters Swim Team I am on works out together a few days a week, and we've all been swimming under Coach Ken for more than fifteen years. We hurry in to make our 1:00 p.m. workout time, swim our laps, have a few laughs, bitch and moan about a hard set Coach Ken gave us, and show up rain or shine, year after year. We know each other's names, if we are married or not, if we have kids, and basic job descriptions, but that's about it. After all, there's not a whole lot of time for chitchat when your head is underwater or when you are done with a set and gasping for air. We are so used to seeing each other in our little Speedo swimsuits that we barely recognize each other with our clothes on. These are people I might not ordinarily have anything in common with, except that I see them more often than some of my closest friends.

One of my team mates is Linda, a pretty, bubbly, mother of five who comes to swim after driving her kids all over town, doing the grocery shopping, and getting her nonfat Cafè au Lait from Peet's Coffee. Linda is a typical Mill Valley mom, someone who I wouldn't think I would have a lot in common with and relate to very well. To me, she looks like she has it all, except that her teenage son, Owen, is dying of cancer.

Linda sends out emails to all of her friends, including her swimming family. She tells us about the hospital visits, the numerous chemo treatments, and Owen's ups and downs. She talks about trying to balance what she is feeling with running an active family that has its own needs. And still she swims. I swim in the same lane with her and wonder how she can hold it together and not lash out at God for this incredible injustice, or curl up in a fetal position under the covers. She does admit, in her emails, that the idea of lying on a beach in Acapulco with a tall margarita sounds really good. But instead she takes it day by day, and swims when she can.

I remember when my mother was dying of cancer in the convalescent hospital. I would look out the window and see the school bus show up every morning, see the daily routines of all the families, see people going to work, and wonder how life could just go on when I was going through this horrible event. But then I got it...life does go on. Every day the sun will rise and set, babies will be born, and people will die. Maybe the challenge of life is just to learn how to surf the waves...and just keep swimming.

Epilogue to this story:

It was six months ago when I first wrote about Owen and Linda. During the ensuing months there were many hospital visits, times of hope where it looked like he was getting better, and times of fear when it looked like the cancer was winning. Eventually, over time, the cancer won out, and Owen died on October 21, 2008. The day I found out, I remember hearing the news and crying in the water as I swam my laps. It just seemed so unfair. I went to his memorial service where five hundred adults and kids joined together in a park in Mill Valley to cry, sing, and share about this remarkable kid who made such a huge difference in his thirteen years of being on the planet.

"In three words I can sum up everything I've learned
about life—it goes on." — ROBERT FROST

Life Goes On

Words & Music: Karen Drucker

My faith has been challenged to the core.
The things that I was so sure of, I just can't count on anymore.
But a new strength and wisdom has risen from my soul.
Each day brings new lessons and this much I do know....

    CHORUS:
    That life goes on. I'll keep walking over mountains.
    I'll keep walking through the valleys, 'cause life goes on.
    And now I see, I don't have any answers.
    I'll just take it day by day, 'cause life goes on.

I get so scared of life's uncertainty.
I keep tryin' to hold on to the people I love.
Sometimes I forget God is holding me.
Love is surrounding me, it's all part of the journey.

    CHORUS

I wish I had the power or a magic wand,
to take away all the suffering and pain.
There's nothing I can do but have an open mind.
Control is an illusion, we're all living on God's time.

    CHORUS

No matter if I'm happy, no matter if I'm sad,
no matter if I'm good or bad.
The sun will come up, the sun will go down,
we're on this planet just spinning around.
The seasons will change, people will die.
Babies are born and we question why.
How life goes on, that life goes on.

CHAPTER 34

On My Way

Whmen I was younger, I thought that the way you got from where you were to where you wanted to be was just a straight line. You set your goal, you state your intention, and you just do it. Simple. But as I grew up, I learned that life just doesn't always work that way.

In 1989, I was part of a wonderful group of five other women who set a goal to be the first American Women's Relay Team to swim the English Channel. After years of being a competitive pool swimmer and then switching to open water swimming as an adult, this would be my own personal Mt. Everest. We trained both individually and as a group for about six months. We swam every day, in all kinds of weather, building up to be able to swim an hour at a time for the relay. We even swam a few times after dark, attaching florescent sticks to the backs of our suits so we could be seen if we had to swim in the middle of the night. (Besides my fear of having to swim through a cluster of jelly fish in the Channel, swimming at night was my next biggest fear. Luckily for me we started in the early morning, and we never even saw any jelly fish!)

We raised the funds to fly there, and filled out the extensive forms required by the English Channel Swimming Association. Everything had to be done quite properly to be considered "legitimate" by the association if you wanted to be recognized by them. We then hired a crusty, jaded fisherman named Willy, who had an old funky boat and who also had a track record of making many successful crossings.

After preparing for months, we were ready physically and mentally to swim the twenty- two mile stretch from Dover, England, to Calais, France. Imagine my surprise when I learned you don't actually swim straight across, which means it's not twenty-two miles but closer to thirty-two or even more. The trick to getting from Dover to Calais is about catching the tides, knowing when and where to be at the exact moment when the tide will turn. You either get to ride that tide, or it will work against you. We wound up going in a zigzag all the way across the Channel because if you actually tried to swim straight across you would never make it.

At one point as I started swimming in a direction that felt like I was going out to sea, I had to trust that the pilot really knew what he was doing. I had to let go of control, have faith, surrender, and trust. Ah, those magic words: surrender and trust. Ten hours and fifty-four minutes after leaving the beach at Dover, England, our final swimmer touched down on the beach of Calais, France. We now had the record as the first American women to swim the Channel, and also had the fastest time that year for a woman's relay team.

I have looked at those occasions in my life when I just let go and trusted and had faith, and how when I did so a kind of current (be it a person, situation, new job) would come along and take me for an easy ride. When that happened, I didn't have to push. I could just let go and be swept along, eventually reaching some new destination. Then there were the times when I would try to control everything. How hard and painful that would feel in comparison!

I am always amazed when I facilitate at women's retreats that the theme so often emerges of how our greatest tragedies or disappointments led to the life or the path we are on now. It is what I call the "zigzag" approach to life. I have sat in circles with women and felt my heart open as I listened to countless stories that left us all weeping—stories of losing a child, being raped, having cancer, or the death of a loved one. But it was because of these circumstances that we were all here in this circle looking at how we were shaped, molded, guided, to begin a new path or choose a new life.

My friend Joan Borysenko is the perfect example of this zigzag path. She had a prestigious job at Harvard Medical Center, one she had worked long and hard to get and to keep. Yet after years of stress and hospital politics she had wanted out. Like so many women, her heart said one thing but her rational mind said another. She stayed at that job, not knowing how to break the cycle. Then one night, while leading her support group for HIV-AIDS patients, she casually mentioned how you can never know the time of your death. "Heck I could die tonight," she said to the group. As if God were listening and mistaking her statement as an intention, she smashed her car head-on into a tree, slamming her face into the steering wheel and ripping off her nose. Later, when she was in the hospital, having undergone emergency surgery, she realized this was her spiritual two-by-four wake up call. She has said that it's never good to make decisions while heavily medicated, but that's what she did. She called her boss and quit right then and there. Since that time she has gone on to have an amazing career as a bestselling author, speaker, and workshop facilitator.

The hardest thing I have ever had to do is walk the path of cancer with both my parents. Sitting in gray, drab, sterile hospital "lounges" while my mother underwent her three-hour chemo infusions, I would be amazed that the only "entertainment" for her to focus on was an old TV in the corner that I swear was set to play nothing but cheesy old game shows and *Bonanza* reruns. What about the idea of providing positive, uplifting music, books, magazines, inspirational authors on tape, things that would affirm life and infuse the patients with hope and strength? As hard as all of that time was, I feel that it gave me a deeper purpose of creating life-affirming music, especially for people going through cancer, recovery, and domestic violence situations...anyone who needs to hear a positive message through music.

As I look back at my own zigzag path, there is no way I would have thought that the various disappointments, setbacks, or pain in my life would lead me to who I am today. My life certainly has not been a straight line, but I am open to wherever the tide will take me next.

"Do not resist events that move you out of your comfort zone,
espcially when your comfort zone was not all that comfortable."
ALAN COHEN

On My Way

Words: Karen Drucker & Debra Turner
Music: Karen Drucker

It kinda looks like I'm making this trip by myself,
and I don't know just where it will lead.
Although I feel so alone I've got something inside,
that lets me know I've got all that I need.
When I started on my journey I didn't know what I'd see.
But I am here today, and that's enough for me.

CHORUS:
To be on my way. I'm on my way. I'm on my way.

Now I'm not sure if this road is the one I should take,
although I've seen it so clear in my mind.
And though I doubt and I fear and I worry I know,
that I'm destined to get there on time.
When I started on my journey I didn't know who I'd be.
But I am here today, and that's enough for me.

CHORUS

CHAPTER 35

Let It Shine

Remember when you were young and you would get little stickers with hearts or flowers or happy faces on your homework when you did a good job? I had a calendar that had a gazillion stickers for every event. Birthdays. Vacations. Days off from school. Whenever there was some kind of important event, there was a sticker that went with it, and I delighted in placing my sticker on the corresponding date.

I have begun that process again. My friend, Deb, whom I swim with on my Masters Swim Team, has inspired me to rethink my old relationship with stickers. I swim about three or four days a week and some days I just show up and go through the paces, using the "workout" as justification to have extra French fries at lunch. Well, Deb doesn't see it that way. For her, every workout is an opportunity for a sticker that she can put on her calendar acknowledging that she bettered her time, lost a pound or two, or increased the number of days she swam that week.

At first I just thought that this practice of acknowledging herself was cute but that it wasn't relevant to me. I showed up—what more do you want? However, after she gifted me with my own calendar and little custom stickers that she designed and printed, well, I had to try it. She made me stickers with little hearts, goddesses coming out of seashells, happy faces, and mermaids. My system was simple: a blue dot if I swam, a green dot if I walked that day, a purple one for biking, a mermaid for swimming in the Bay, a goddess if I did something really fun, and a happy face if I had a really good workout. Soon I began a new relationship with the big clock at the side of the pool that times our laps. I had just ignored it previously, but now that same clock had a whole new meaning. I could actually get a happy face if I bettered my time. I now lived for placing those happy face stickers on my calendar!

I began to look at my whole life differently because of this simple, little game. How much was I acknowledging other events in my life, both the big things and the little things? I have a daily practice of doing a gratitude blessing every morning, being grateful for the people in my life. How many times was I putting myself into those blessings? How much was I acknowledging what I was doing in my life? It felt kind of selfish and wrong on some level to me, and yet the more I did it, the more I started to think I could tackle other areas of my life that I had put on the back burner. Deb didn't show her calendar to the world every time she accomplished something. Actually, no one was aware of her ritual except me. However, I knew that when she broke her best time by two seconds that she was thrilled and that she was going to run home and put a happy face sticker on her calendar that day.

So what do YOU need to give yourself a sticker for? What do YOU need to acknowledge yourself for?

I do an exercise in one of my workshops where I ask people to walk around the room and "brag" to each other. I ask them to tell people about how wonderful they are, what they have accomplished in their lives, or what qualities in themselves they are the most proud of. I tell everyone the rules: You have to say it in one sentence, you have to talk to as many people as you can within three minutes, and you can't repeat the same thing to any person. Upon hearing the directions, I have seen people glaze over and turn an interesting shade of green. If I had said let's all discuss what is wrong with our lives or ourselves, many of us could go for hours with our old stories and get agreement on how it's all so unfair. But no. Here you have to "brag." Something that a good girl like me was taught not to do.

My mother told me that when I was about six years old, I would do a nightly "show" where I would stand on the little raised platform of our fireplace and proceed to tap dance and sing to anyone who would listen to what my day in kindergarten was like. This continued for years until I started getting the message, sometimes subtly with a look from my mother or a statement from my father, that I was "too much." These soon became a list of statements that I would embody and live by:

"Don't call attention to yourself."

"Boys won't like you if you are smarter or funnier than them."

"Don't be too loud, too big, too much."

"Don't stand on a soap box."

"Don't be a Sarah Bernhardt" (meaning don't be dramatic and feel whatever you are feeling).

What was once a shining light of energy, life, and enthusiastic joy, slowly got dimmer and dimmer. Add to the mix teenage insecurity, self-doubt, acne, braces, un-hip curly hair, and I became the shy girl in the corner who was known as the good student who swam.

And yet there was a light deep down inside of me, wanting to be reignited. It would take years of personal inner work to reconnect with that flame and feel the joy that little girl in me used to feel.

"As we let our light shine, we unconsciously give other people permission to do the same." — MARIANNE WILLIAMSON

The truth is we are all meant to shine in our own unique way, no matter what that way is. It doesn't matter what occupation we have, the color of our skin, our ethnicity, or our religious background. We have all been given a life force, and I believe it is our birthright and responsibility to discover our light, to feed and nurture it, and to allow it to grace everyone we meet. Of course, we can find a million and one reasons why we shouldn't, from all of the reasons we heard as children to the fear of what people will think or say. However, it all comes down to joy—our own joy. Joy is what feeds us, makes us happy, and allows our light to shine. Ernest Holmes says, "Joy is the emotion excited by the expectancy of good." The more we allow our individual light to shine, the more other people will allow their light to shine. Like the quotation says, we give each other "permission to do the same."

Recently, I was on the rental car shuttle bus in Kansas City. Melinda, the bus driver, was shining so brightly that our ride from the rental car terminal to the airport was the highlight of my whole trip. This woman was doing "ministry." She got on the microphone and informed us that this was "her bus" and that we were all going to leave our stresses behind and feel taken care of for the seven-minute drive to the airport. She wanted to make sure we were happy and filled up with good feelings before we left "her bus." We were clearly a group of stressed-out, rushed, and impatient travelers, yet she had us all laughing, smiling, and connecting with her seven minute "show." She did this so well that when I saw a few of my bus-mates on my flight back to San Francisco, we all waved and laughed as if we were old friends.

A totally unexpected bright light was the "mixologist" whom I met when my sister, Tina, and I were on a weekend getaway. We had about thirty minutes before we could be seated for dinner at this wonderful spa that we had treated ourselves to. Tina had wanted to go into the bar for a glass of wine while we waited. We walked into the bar and memories flooded my mind. There was a female pianist in the corner, singing songs of love to no one in particular. The dark room, the smell of old, stale cigarette smoke, and the couples huddling in the corner, all combined to bring me back to my years singing in bars. I immediately wanted to leave because it was just too depressing. My sister promised me we would sit at the bar for just a minute, order our drinks, and then go wait outside. The bar turned out to be a martini bar.

Since I had never even had a martini and since I was on vacation, I agreed.

All of a sudden it was as if a spotlight had come on and Nick, our bartender, informed that us he was the #1 "mixologist" in the country. After telling us that his specialty martinis have won numerous awards, he started his "show." He told us about the various drinks, selling them like he was selling a shiny new car, and got the eight of us who were sitting at the bar laughing, talking with one another, and connecting.

Ah, that favorite word of mine: connecting. We were eight strangers with nothing in common, who had just come in to pass the time before dinner. Because of Nick and his joy, passion, and enthusiasm about making martinis, we were now all connected, watching his show and becoming totally engrossed in the world of martinis. I had a martini with a Hawaiian theme. It was made with pineapple and coconut, and with one of those little paper umbrellas sticking out of the side. It was delicious, but even more so because of Nick's show.

Another example of a bright light shining is John, who runs the food service at Unity Village in Kansas City, Missouri, and who happens to be an amazing singer. In the midst of the chaos and noise from all of the people in the classes and retreats who were coming in for lunch, John has been known to suddenly walk into the center of the room and break into song. He sings show tunes, opera—anything that will get everyone singing and clapping along. He has been known to serenade unsuspecting customers while they are sipping their soup. When this happens, everyone stops, listens, and connects as we all put down our forks and wildly applaud this act of selfless service.

My favorite shining light is Rudy, a toll taker on the Golden Gate Bridge. Whenever I get in Rudy's lane, coming into San Francisco, I know it will be a great day. For the fifteen to twenty seconds he has to take my money and give me a receipt before I drive away, he always comes up with something that brings me joy, some kind of little affirmation or compliment that makes me smile. My favorite one is the rubber fish he waves saying, "Go swimmingly through your day!" as he hands me my receipt. I can't imagine how many people Rudy has blessed over the years with his unique ministry.

All the people I have just mentioned I call "twinklers." They are people who shine, who give of themselves and allow their light to shine on everyone they meet. They seem to embody one of my favorite quotes from Charles Fillmore, who said at age 94, "I fairly sizzle with zeal and enthusiasm and spring forth with a mighty faith to do the things that ought to be done by me." I get inspired by people like them and want to know what their secret is. Whenever I see them or experience their brightness, I feel it gives me permission to shine my light a little brighter.

" First, think.Second, believe. Third, dream. And finally, dare."
WALT DISNEY

Let It Shine

Words & Music: Karen Drucker

SONG INSPIRED BY ALAN COHEN
from his book *Dare to Be Yourself*

I'm gonna be the first on the dance floor, the first to raise my hand.
The first to state my opinion, the first to take a stand.
I won't play it safe and wait for a sign,
I'm gonna throw myself out there and let my light shine.

CHORUS:
Let it shine, let it shine,
I let my big bright brilliant beam of radiant light shine.

I'll be on "Oprah" and "Conan," "60 Minutes" and "The View."
They'll all be talking about me and all the things I do.
I'll be the one who sets the bar, the one who's in the know.
Vogue will come to me to see where fashion trends will go.

CHORUS
For too many years I hid my light fearing I was too much and who
I was just wasn't right.
Then I heard this voice from within and up above saying,
"You're here to be a shining light and give and receive love."

So now I'm going for my dreams, nothing's in my way.
"Carpe Diem" is my mantra, I practice kindness every day.
I take time to connect, take time to have fun.
I wanna know I've used up every drop before my life is done.

CHORUS

I am a woman of power, a woman of grace.
The life that I've lived is in every wrinkle on my face.
I love myself so I can love you too,
I know when we're connected there ain't nothin' we can't do.

> CHORUS:
> Let it shine, let it shine,
> I let my big bright brilliant beam of radiant light shine.

CHAPTER 36

There's Enough

A Taoist story tells of a farmer who had an old horse for tilling his fields. One day the horse ran away, and when all the farmer's neighbors sympathized with the man over his bad luck, the farmer replied, "Bad luck? Good luck? Who knows?" A week later the horse returned with a herd of wild horses, and this time the neighbors congratulated the farmer on his good luck. His reply was, "Good luck? Bad luck? Who knows?" Then, as the farmer's son was attempting to tame one of the wild horses, he fell off its back and broke his leg. Everyone thought this was very bad luck—but not the farmer, whose only reaction was, "Bad luck? Good luck? Who knows?" A few weeks later military officials came to the village to draft all the young men into the army. When they saw the farmer's son with his broken leg they passed him by. The neighbors once again congratulated the farmer on how well things had turned out. All he said was "Good luck? Bad luck? Who knows?"

When I look back on my life, and all the stories that I have told in this book, I realize how this expression of "Good luck, Bad luck, Who Knows?" is the phrase that has shaped my life. There must have been something in me that knew that taking a risk, letting go of the shore and its safety, would lead me to my next adventure. I never knew where I was being led, and I can guarantee there were times when I was kicking and screaming as I made myself push away and float into the mystery of the unknown. And here I am doing it again by writing this book.

If only I had read this Taoist story when I was a young woman I think I could have saved myself from years of pain, tears, and therapy. "If only"...two words that can either lead to regret or learning. When I play the "If Only" game I am amazed at the results that led me to where I am now:

If only I had been the "pretty girl" in school and was wildly popular—I don't know if I would have developed my sense of humor and compassion for anyone who is different and feels like an outsider.

If only I was successful at being a Hollywood singer/songwriter with a recording deal—I don't know if I would have found the musical path that has filled my heart and soul.

If only my parents had not died from cancer—I don't know if I would have found the calling and vision of writing healing music for people going through this process.

If only I had had more success as a private party musician (I could still be singing "La Bamba" and "Feelings" at a bride's wedding who would now be my granddaughter!)— I don't know if I would have ever started singing in New Thought churches.

If only I had not been dumped by a boyfriend—I would have never found my husband.

If only I had not been fired from my first job—I might still be scooping the poop at Beverly Hills Ponyland!

And on it goes...maybe that is the lesson for me, to allow and surrender to what is happening and to trust that this could be a "recalculation" from the path that I was convinced was mine, to the path that would ultimately serve my highest good. Maybe, just maybe, Spirit has another, bigger, more fulfilling plan or vision for me, and I can just let go of the shore and ride the tide. It's taken me years to learn to accept the process of being in the mystery, to stop thinking it's all about getting "there," wherever "there" is.

My good friend, Reverend David Ault, shared with me a great example of this concept. To celebrate and mark his 50th birthday, he did the centuries-old pilgrimage known as the Camino de Santiago (The Way of Saint James), walking from the small French border village of Saint Jean Pied de Port, over the Pyrenees, and across the northern rim of Spain to the city of Santiago de Compostela, a total of 500 miles. Thousands upon thousands of people have made the pilgrimage on this famous path and there are many books telling of the adventure. One challenge every walking pilgrim faces is getting a bed for the night in the hostels (or albergues) that exist throughout the various towns and villages along the path. With only a certain amount of beds available, whoever arrives first is guaranteed a bed for the night. David began noticing that some of his fellow walkers made this spectacular life-changing event all about "getting there" — making sure they had a bed for the night and that their physical needs were met. They had an intensity to their walking as if they were in a race to break through the ribbon at the finish line and win a gold medal. Soon David found himself stressing about the daily bed ritual and quickening his pace to keep up with the rest. In a moment of "losing it" along the side of the road after days of this pressure, David then experienced another moment of "getting it." When he allowed himself to just "be" and enjoy the process, to trust that there is always enough, and that he was taken care of, the Camino became a life changing experience for him. There was always a place for him to sleep, always enough food to eat, and always enough time to "get there."

As I continue on my path and keep affirming there is enough and that every event or situation is an opportunity to keep my heart open and grow, I am forever changing. I have been graced by this path and continue to be a willing student. If I can keep singing my songs, telling my stories, and having people listen, then that's enough for me.

"Enough is not a number or condition. It is a state of mind."
ALAN COHEN

There's Enough
Words: Karen Drucker
Music: Karen Drucker & John Hoy

There's enough time to do all that I want to do.
There's enough time to "be" and do it all.
Whenever I look inside, that's when I realize,
there's enough time, there's enough time, there's enough time.
Time, there is enough. Time, there is enough.

There's enough love to give, there's enough love to receive.
There's enough love to give and to receive.
I open my heart, that's the place to start.
There's enough love, there's enough love, there's enough love.
Love, there is enough. Love, there is enough.

There's enough joy in my heart, I choose joy every day.
There's enough joy for all of us to shine.
When I allow joy to be, it becomes a part of me.
There's enough joy, there's enough joy, there's enough joy.
Joy, there is enough. Joy, there is enough.

ABOUT THE AUTHOR

KAREN DRUCKER

✔ She has been a singing mermaid, a tap dancing/singing casket, and literally was "elevator music" when she was hired to sing and play piano in a moving elevator.

✔ She first became interested in music while she was the baby-sitter for singer/songwriter Carole King's children.

✔ She swam the English Channel with five other women, becoming the first American women's relay team to make a successful crossing.

✔ She rode her bike from San Francisco to Los Angeles in the AIDS ride.

✔ She walked from Santa Barbara to Malibu in the Avon Breast Cancer Walk.

✔ She had her own TV show when she was 21.

✔ She was awarded an Honorary Doctorate in music from the United Centers for Spiritual Living.

✔ But her most impressive achievement was winning the International Tarzan calling contest when she 13.

Karen Drucker has recorded thirteen CDs of her original inspirational music. She has won numerous awards for her songwriting and volunteer work for performing and producing shows for organizations in need. She has been a professional comedienne, lead her own band for corporate events, and has been the music director for three different New Thought churches, as well as music director and "music weaver" for many spiritual conferences and retreats.

She sings, speaks and leads workshops at women's retreats, mind-body & health conferences and various churches around the country. She has worked with authors like Joan Borysenko, Alan Cohen, Cheri Huber, SARK, Mary Manin Morrissey, and many others.

Karen has been called "a master of communicating presence and spirituality through music." She loves making music, making a difference, and touching hearts.

KAREN DRUCKER DISCOGRAPHY

Karen Drucker	Cassette	1989
One of a Kind Love	CD	1993
Songs of the Spirit	CD	1999
Hold on to Love	CD	2000
Songs of the Spirit 2	CD	2001
Beloved	CD	2002
All About Love	CD	2004
Songs of the Spirit 3	CD	2005
Shine	CD	2007
Songs of the Spirit 4	CD	2009

Compilation CDs

Chants & Sing-alongs	Songbook/CD	2006
The Heart of Healing	Compilation CD	2006
Power of Women	Compilation CD	2008
Let Go of the Shore	Compilation CD	2010
In the Stillness	Compilation CD	2010

CDs for Organizations

Permission to Play	Compilation CD	2006
A Retreat of My Own	Compilation CD	2008
A Time to Heal	Compilation CD	2009

For CDs, songbooks and other information:
www.karendrucker.com

INDEX OF SONGS

Part One: I Can Do It

CHAPTER / SONG	FROM THE CD
1. I Can Do It	Let Go of the Shore
2. Just Do It	Songs of the Spirit 3
3. We Are the Ones	Shine
4. Prosperity	Songs of the Spirit 2
5. I've Got the Power	All About Love
6. The Call of Something More	Let Go of the Shore
7. This or Something Better	Songs of the Spirit 3
8. Taming My Inner Critic	All About Love
9. I Don't Have to Be Perfect	Let Go of the Shore
10. One Small Step	Hold On to Love
11. I Lost the Right to Sing the Blues	Hold On to Love
12. Relax, Let Go	Songs of the Spirit 3
13. I Allow, I Surrender	Songs of the Spirit 4
14. Face of God	Songs of the Spirit 2
15. N-O Is My New Yes	All About Love
16. We Are All Angels	Songs of the Spirit 2

Part Two: What Does Your Heart Have to Say?

17. Calling All Angels	All About Love
18. Listen to the Children	Hold On to Love
19. Christmas Lullaby	All About Love
20. My Religion Is Kindness	Beloved
21. You Are My Family	All About Love
22. You Are Loved	All About Love
23. Breathe	Beloved
24. Gentle With Myself	Songs of the Spirit 3
25. In Beauty May I Walk	Songs of the Spirit 4
26. Lighten Up	Beloved
27. Let Go of the Shore	Let Go of the Shore

Part Three: Let It Shine

28. What Would Love Do?	All About Love
29. I Am Healed	Songs of the Spirit 4
30. Feel It	Shine
31. Three Little Words	Shine
32. Permission to Play	Let Go of the Shore
33. Life Goes On	All About Love
34. On My Way	Hold On to Love
35. Let It Shine	Shine
36. There's Enough	Songs of the Spirit 3

ABOUT THE ILLUSTRATOR

Brian Narelle began gag cartooning at the age of eight. No one ever told him to stop. So he didn't. His cartoons have appeared in books, calendars, magazines, web sites, and on numerous restaurant napkins. He's worked for *Sesame Street*, Lucasfilm, and Pixar as well as starring in the sci-fi cult film *Dark Star* and the Discovery Channel's children's series *Bingo and Molly*. His animated TV commercial for KGB Radio gave birth to the *San Diego Chicken*. In recent years he's been teaching cartooning at the Charles M. Schulz Museum in California.

As a screenwriter he has written dozens of films to empower children, as well as commercials, corporate videos, children's television, animated shorts and PBS Specials, collecting Cine Gold Eagle, Annie and Emmy Awards.

In the end he always returns to cartooning, which he defines as, "Truth, graphically conveyed with humor, using the least possible amount of ink."

www.briannarelle.com

Printed in the USA
CPSIA information can be obtained
at www.ICGtesting.com
JSHW082203140824
68134JS00014B/409